Yale Studies in Hermeneutics

Hermeneutics, Religion, and Ethics

Hans-Georg Gadamer
Translated by Joel Weinsheimer

Yale University Press   New Haven and London

Set in Caslon type by Tseng Information Systems.
Printed in the United States of America.

Library of Congress Cataloging-in-Publication Data
Gadamer, Hans Georg, 1900–
Hermeneutics, religion, and ethics /
Hans-Georg Gadamer ;
translated by Joel Weinsheimer.
p.   cm. — (Yale studies in hermeneutics)
Includes bibliographical references and index.
ISBN: 978-0-300-17830-2
1. Hermeneutics.   2. Religion.   3. Ethics.
I. Title.   II. Series.
B3248.G33H47   1999
121'.686—dc21   99-13088
CIP

A catalogue record for this book is
available from the British Library.

The paper in this book meets the guidelines
for permanence and durability of the Committee
on Production Guidelines for Book Longevity of
the Council on Library Resources.

Contents

TRANSLATOR'S PREFACE

Readers familiar with *Truth and Method* (1960) will not be surprised to learn that in the years immediately preceding and following the publication of his magnum opus, Gadamer returned again and again to the questions about religion and ethics that figure so prominently there. The essays here selected from the *Gesammelte Werke* and translated into English for the first time show Gadamer probing more deeply into the hermeneutic significance of these subjects.

Never claiming to write about religion as a theologian, Gadamer approaches the subject from a secular direction, as it bears on his life's project of conceptualizing understanding generally. This generality should not be taken to imply, however, that Gadamer dismisses religious hermeneutics as just another case of hermeneutics in general or that he succumbs to the humanist tendency to reduce the divine to the human. From its earliest recorded mentions, Western hermeneutics has always applied both to scriptures or quasi-scriptures (see Plato's *Ion*) and to human discourse (see Aristotle's *Peri Hermeneuein*), and Gadamer offers good hermeneutic reasons to preserve this breadth.

The interpretation of religious texts, he shows, is irreducible, because it has something to teach us not just about theological hermeneutics, but about secular interpretation as well. For instance, the claim of divine meaning to be the same yesterday, today, and forever seems at first to be a special and, from a historical point of view, dubious attribute of the sacred text alone. Gadamer shows, however, that every kind of interpretation, and not just that informed by faith, must ineluctably posit the inviolability and self-sameness of meaning. Without such a dialectical counterbalance to the self-difference of meaning evident in secular interpretation, even nonreligious interpretation necessarily falls into what Gadamer calls "hermeneutic nihilism"—the premise that every new reading is a new creation—which amounts to the denial that interpretation and understanding are possible at all. The real problem of hermeneutics, then, is to think difference and sameness, the secular and the religious, together.

Not just the interpretation of sacred texts is Gadamer's concern in the essays that follow; the more general claim of religion has implications for hermeneutic inquiry as well. If reason, as viewed by the Enlightenment, represents the unboundedness of human aspiration and the unlimited possibilities open to thought and endeavor, religion (according to Gadamer) foregrounds "the boundary situations of guilt and death, where human Dasein finds through its own experience its powerlessness before the power of fate" (p. 3). We who live in the post-atomic, even post-technological age, have become disillusioned "concerning the power of human beings over nature, and perhaps, even more, concerning the control of human suffering" (p. 125). Whether in the realm of mechanical engineering or social engineering, each failure of control, each confrontation with the limits of human possibility, points toward a domain that exceeds it. In the face of tragedy and the power of fate, we experience the fundamental appeal of religion and the ultimate hollowness of an idealistic philosophy that enshrines human will and consciousness.

The divine is an enduringly powerful way of thinking about what exceeds consciousness. It is not Gadamer's preferred way, as it was for Kierkegaard, among others; but the divine figures very prominently among the whole array of concepts that Gadamer deploys in his multifaceted critique of modern subjectivity. From the acknowledgment that we are not in control of ourselves or the world in which we live, the acknowledgment of the divine is only one step away. "[I]t is precisely the experience of the limits of freedom—of ability and of knowledge, the fact that all of us are determined by supraindividual powers, which brings into question the modern presupposition that the individual . . . represents the *ens realissimum* of all beings" (p. 16). More real than the individual, in Gadamer's view, is "supraindividual being" (p. 14). This is represented by the supreme being, to be sure; but it is also exemplified by other modes of being that (no less than the divine) lie outside the circumference of human consciousness and control: one instance is what Hegel terms "objective mind"—all the institutions of family structure, language, and community life that are of human origin, certainly, but that have no individual creator and exercise uncontrollable influence on individual destinies. Often Gadamer terms all this not "objective mind" but rather "life," "world," or just "being," since being in this sense (as in the case of the supreme being) is always supraindividual.

By the *polis*, for example, Gadamer understands a mode of being, not consensus of individual views or a collectivity of individuals formed by a social contract. These latter are modern subjectivist notions. For the Greeks, by contrast, the polis means "what is common to us all . . . to the true form of which everyone is at all times answerable" (p. 32). Less the product of consciousness than its condition, the polis exemplifies a "dimension of things that we share" and to which we belong (p. 117). "Our actions," Gadamer writes, "are *situated within* the horizon of the polis, and thus our choice of what needs to be done spreads out into the whole of our external social being" (p. 32; emphasis added). "Situated within" is how Gadamer describes our relation to (supraindividual) being: he does not locate what is beyond consciousness in a metaphysical elsewhere, above and apart from the world. Quite the contrary, it is precisely the being that we are "situated within" that, however near, is also most beyond us.

Gadamer's resolute insistence on the this-worldliness of being, we might suppose, stamps him as a secular philosopher. Yet this supposition is complicated by the fact that he views this world as itself beyond, and correlatively the divine comes to be conceived as much nearer than we are wont to think it. For the Greeks, as Gadamer shows in explicating passages from Xenophanes and Parmenides, the divine

> is present for those who are acquainted with it [*innesein,* also "to be aware of"]. In understanding this, all appeals to an idealistic tradition are misplaced. [Greek religion] does not begin from "thought"; what it is about is being—that is, the way what exists is, and this includes its being such that one is acquainted with it as present. That is the meaning of *noein:* the immediate exposure to the There. (p. 47)

"Immediate exposure"—or knowing by being "situated within" —is not limited to the Greek conception of the divine, however; it is very much a part of Christianity as well. Our being within God, rather than distant from an otherworldly divine, receives expression in a memorable passage of *Acts:*

> Then Paul stood in the midst of Mars' hill and said, Ye men of Athens, I perceive that in all things ye are too superstitious. . . . God that made the world and all things therein . . . [is] not far from every one of us; for in him we live, and move, and have

our being; as certain of your own poets have said.
(17:22–7)

Common to Greek and Christian religion, then, is a sense of God's immediacy to us and the corollary notion of our being within God. God is at once most near and far, at the same time best known and least, because "the divine," in the language of faith, names the whole of which we are part.

These same themes figure largely in Gadamer's conception of philosophical ethics as well, even though the latter is not specially based on religious principles. Since Gadamer does not dichotomize reason and religion in the manner of the Enlightenment, his essays move from *mythos* to *logos* and back in a way that bespeaks their indissoluble unity. In this respect, he follows a paradigm set by Greek thought. "Plato's myths of the soul and its fate, and of the rule of the gods over the course of the world," Gadamer writes, "illustrate this unity [of mythos and logos] through their baroque mixture of styles, where the festiveness of sacred language is wedded to the Ionic spirit of reflection" (p. 82). This same mixture obtains in the realm of ethics as well. Again following the pattern set by Greek thought, especially the Socratic tradition that identifies virtue and knowledge, Gadamer discerns a connection between *ethos* and logos, "between the adult's becoming socialized through education and training and the logos of justification" (p. 143). Briefly put, rational reflection about the good cannot and need not be prescinded from life. Ethical knowledge is knowing from within, because in this, as in every instance, knowing is indissolubly tied to being.

That is one way of phrasing the "universality of hermeneutics," one of Gadamer's most controversial claims. Ethics repeatedly rivets his attention because it paradigmatically symbolizes that universality, yet the hermeneutical insistence on the bond of knowing and being also complicates Gadamer's conception of ethics. The indivisibility of reflective ethics from unreflective ethos renders both of them so full of tension as to be almost paradoxical. On one hand, Gadamer wants to do full justice to ethics as a form of knowing. He wants to preserve the cognitive character of ethics understood as a species of philosophy and so belonging to "the logos of justification." Insofar as we can explain and legitimate our ethical decisions, knowing what is morally right must count as a kind of genuine knowledge. On the other hand, Gadamer must do equal justice to the fact that ethics is indivisible from ethos; and ethos—specifically "the state of being arising from training"—like all being, is "beyond us." More precisely, ethos is present to us but not as an object of consciousness. Ethics is a kind of reflection, then, but it is tied to ethos, and ethos is a kind of being, hence non-reflective. Just this paradox gives hermeneutics its task, that of "mediating ethos and philosophical ethics" (p. 68).

Moral decisions are always "situated within" an ethos that is unjustified and in need of no justification, but rather given, evident, and so patent as to obviate dispute. This obviousness explains the obligatory character of moral principles, their claim to obedience. Lotze's value-based ethics, in Gadamer's view, does not do sufficient justice to the binding quality of ethical obligation, because Lotze defines the realm of value as that comprehending morality and beauty, and he ascribes obligation not to the aesthetic but to fact. Gadamer does just the opposite, emphasizing the truth-claim of the beautiful and indeed considering the neo-Kantian fact/value distinction "pointless . . . after the dogmatism of the concept of 'fact' has been critiqued by theory of science, hermeneutics, and ideology critique" (p. 58).

If the rootedness of moral principles in ethos explains their binding character, however, it also seems to call the very possibility of a philosophical ethics into question. Do we really have, say, an obligation to pay our debts? Of course. The unreflectiveness of ethos explains why it is equally impossible to doubt it and to prove it. In the abstract, ethical judgments are intuitively certain, like sensory judgments. Yet ethical disputes exist, and they are rarely disputes about the obvious. In such cases, where the "logos of justification" is required, arguments can be made, and the decisions taken can be assessed as more, or less, reasonable. In these cases, too, the reasons adduced are themselves grounded in ethos, and such grounding is possible because ethos is not merely unreflective. It is rather a prereflective awareness—capable of becoming the object of self-conscious reflection, but not originating in that way or necessarily aspiring to it.

When ethical reflection or self-conscious reflection on the good does occur, Gadamer argues, this "can be nothing but the mere self-clarification of the determinations of concrete ethos" (p. 74). Notice that he does not say, "ethics clarifies ethos." Rather, ethos is self-clarifying. Ethics itself is an element immanent within ethos and does not advene from without. As Gadamer writes, "practical philosophy can do nothing but pursue the drive toward knowledge and self-understanding that is always manifesting itself in human actions and decisions" (pp. 150–51). If ethical reflection never breaks free of ethos and is nonetheless genuinely ethical for all that, it is because all "human reason is determined by actual ethos" (p. 74) and is nonetheless reasonable for all that.

Only an Enlightenment antithesis between logos and ethos would imply that reason, because it is always situated within an ethos, cannot therefore be reasonable. That follows only if there is, or at least could be, some state of reason that is situated nowhere, entirely unaffected by ethos. For Gadamer, however, the very absence of unsituated reason explains why "for thinking beings the use of reason is always in need of critique" (pp. 109–10). What obscures and impedes the ongoing work of critique, in fact, is the very supposition that there is, or at least could be, some state of reason that is impartial and complete, not situated within. Gadamer's hermeneutics, however, exposes the very "search for such a thing as a self-deception that ultimately fails to expand an overly narrow ethos" (p. 75). In sum, the dichotomies of the Enlightenment themselves contribute to an artificial narrowness, insofar as they interfere with the impulse to critique, to openness, and hence to reasonableness that hermeneutics discovers in ethos itself.

Joel Weinsheimer

March 1998

I

Kant and the Question of God (1941)

No one who does philosophy nowadays can face the demands
that the question of God makes with anything but dismay.
Does philosophy, then, inquire about God at all? Does the
proposition that God exists involve for philosophers only the
form of a question? Don't we mean by philosophizing an under-
taking of a human being relegated to being responsible for
itself, conscious that its condition is just the opposite of religious certainty? Carrying this to its radical conclusion, Heidegger described philosophy as basically atheism insofar as it
consists in raising one's hand against God, and he rightly emphasized that philosophy knows nothing of "sins" even and
especially when it discerns an essential element of guilt in the
historical movedness of human *Dasein*. This "atheistic" self-
conception of philosophy obviously stands in an intrinsic polemical relation to the Christian understanding of existence—
where Dasein is understood not as autonomous but as a being
indivisible from sin and grace, subject to the call of God, and
experiencing in itself his grace. This distinction is exclusive.
It excludes even the conflict itself, for it is concerned not just
with various understandings of Dasein—from the divine viewpoint or the human—but rather with the various meanings of
that understanding itself. Because it is itself a presupposition,
faith—whether or not it retains the character of a wager—can
never reach the presuppositionlessness that philosophy wagers
and presupposes. What it asserts is this: there is no Christian
philosophy. This assertion can be intended in a Christian sense,
as it was by Luther and as Lutheran orthodoxy has reaffirmed

often enough. But it can also be expressed as the basis of a modern critique of religion, and then it corresponds to the self-consciousness of enlightened humanity.

In truth, however, only a very specific kind of theological and philosophical self-conception carries matters to the extreme of irreconcilable dichotomy. Christian theology in particular is not at all so generally certain about it. It understands the problem as that of natural, as opposed to rational, theology and knowledge of God. Of course, such natural knowledge of God does not plumb the full depths of the Christian mystery. Christianity is *revealed* religion, to be sure, and it belongs to the nature of revelation—that is, of a revealed divine being and his deeds—that its truth and content cannot be understood in another, natural or rational way as well. The Son's act of redemption, like the outpouring of the Holy Ghost, are unacceptable to the natural efforts of reason alone. Yet there is a whole series of Christian (though not exclusively Christian) truths concerning the existence and nature of the divine that can be reached without revelation and thus pertain, for example, to other religious viewpoints as well. Such "rational" theology became in the Christian age an essential—the most important—element of philosophical metaphysics, until philosophy and the philosophical concept of knowledge were subsumed under the norm of knowledge cultivated by the new empirical natural sciences. This amounted to sounding the critical death knell for all speculative theology. Kant brought it to completion. His critique of traditional metaphysics was epoch-making. Ever since, one subject that still occupied progressive minds in the eighteenth century has been banned from philosophy: proofs of God.

No one today expects philosophy to offer proofs of God, or would accept them—despite the attempts of the great Idealist thinkers that have emerged since Kant. In this respect, Kant has remained victorious. Whatever consequences other than critique of religion the general consciousness has drawn from the modern Enlightenment, it still considers the competence of philosophy so limited that no one assigns it the burden of proving the existence of God. Now the proof of God is and remains the presupposition of all rational knowledge of God—at least, after atheistic doubt is awakened. Thus it indeed appears as if modern consciousness—outside faith in the reality of revelation—and philosophy, in which that modern consciousness achieves its full self-realization, have wholly lost the question of God.

Yet it would be wrong to view this loss as liberating philosophy to a state of self-certainty. It is no more sure of itself than a theology in the unshakable fixity of its faith. It is hard for theology to sidestep the demand that faith be harmonized with reason. It retains responsibility for answering the question about natural, rational knowledge of God. Still harder is it for philosophy—at the limits, the boundary situations of guilt and death, where human Dasein finds through its own experience its powerlessness before the power of fate—not to pose the question God. Plato once made the profound remark (in the *Laws* 888c, through the voice of a hoary Athenian, himself an old man) that he had not yet met anyone who had formed the opinion that there are no gods and retained this view into old age. Young people, conscious of unlimited freedom, may be blinded—as they will later be blinded again by the power of time—as if they were afflicted by an infectious disease, the δεινὴ ἀθεότης. What characterizes a spirit with a sound constitution is that it comes back to a recognition of the truth—at least to recognize the existence of the gods, though not always rightly evaluating the significance of their existence for human life. That is, many, according to Plato, stick to their opinion that the gods do not care about us or that they are easily bribed with gifts.

These considerations prepare us for rethinking the distinction established by Kant and basically still valid today: the *atheist* denies absolutely the existence of an ultimate being; the *deist* recognizes one, though not like a human being with free intelligence, but merely as a first cause of the world; the *theist* defines the ground of the world as the creator, by analogy to nature. Life experience, then—this is Plato's tacit opinion—leads humankind to face this problem, thus articulated. So, as we have indicated, the question of God remains a philosophical subject.

Given this situation, it will also become necessary to concern ourselves with the old question regarding the proofs of God. Admittedly, its significance for philosophy today is substantially different from what it was for medieval philosophy, which first worked out these proofs. We will not direct our inquiry within the Christian Church—that is, on the ground provided by revelation—about the possibility of natural, rational knowledge of God; instead, we will pose the philosophical question about being and human Dasein. Our own philosophizing, however, leads us, as historical inquirers, back to the Christian tradition concerning the problem of God. The only philosophy we are acquainted with is that contextualized within the tradition of the Christian West. Even if it consciously divorces itself from the presuppositions of Christian theology, and even if it conceives of itself methodologically as atheistic in that respect, nevertheless its fundamental experiences, as much as the language and concepts with which it interprets them, are influenced by Western Christianity and its spiritual history. That is the first thing. Philosophy itself does not represent the possibility of autonomous questioning and consideration that is the same at all times; instead, it temporalizes itself ever anew in the course of its own history. This obtains even when we do not conceive of philosophy itself as the "final result" of its history (with Hegel), but just take it simply. Second, it follows that the ancient proofs of God, though now unbelievable, sketched out the directions in which the question of God involves philosophical problems still alive today. Thus we will need to examine more closely the proofs of God that emerged in medieval philosophy. To be sure, at issue is not the history of these proofs, or the preparation for them in Greek philosophy, or the gradual elaboration of them in Scholasticism. From the history of these proofs only one thing deserves to be grasped: how interest in the proof of God's existence is connected, with varying emphasis, to knowledge of the essential attributes of God. Anselm in the eleventh century was the first to construct a pure proof of God's existence—Kant called it the "ontological" proof—and it was in the controversy regarding the value of this argument that the other, older arguments were reformulated in a logically strict manner. From a historical perspective as well, Anselm's argument occupies a key position.

Now, we would like to study the proof of God in Kant not only because his critique of it has the ongoing influence that I mentioned in passing, but, primarily, because Kant systematically reduced it to its essential form and, in his critique of the probative value of this "proof," displayed its fundamental rational deficiency. Kant distinguishes, we recall, four kinds of proof: the ontological, the cosmological, the physico-theological, and the ethico-theological. He assigns the first two proofs to transcendental theology and the second two to natural theology. In the first two proofs, it is not particular experiences, but only experience as such or mere concepts that hold the key to the ultimate being. In the other two, by contrast, the experience of the natural or moral order of the world is traced back to its basis, the creator. For that reason, the first two proofs demonstrate only the existence of an ultimate ground or reason for the world (deism), whereas the other two lead to theism—that is, to acceptance of a creator with free intelligence. Now, the intent of the critical inquiry that Kant devotes to these proofs is to show that the logical conclusiveness of the "transcendental" proofs (the ontological and cosmological) is entirely owing to the appearance of being dialectical. From this it follows that with respect to God no speculative (theoretical) knowledge whatever is possible. For the physico-theological proof, however valuable it may seem to be in itself, can be used only in combination with the moral proof, and then only in a postulatory way.

Before examining the validity of this critique, we need to study the content of the arguments more closely. First, Kant called this the "ontological proof" because it proceeds from pure, a priori concepts, without any assistance from experience. It claims that the *ens realissimum*—that is, the being in which the totality of all matters are united—exists by necessity. For otherwise, it would possess all perfections except that of existence. Or, as Kant expresses it, the sublation of this thing, whose concept implies its existence, would contradict its concept. Kant shows, then, that this mode of argument contains within itself a contradictory assumption. The concept of a thing consists of the determinations that constitute its possibility, what I think of it as, its "predicates." "Being," however, is clearly no such real predicate constituting a what-content (thisness). It expresses the mere givenness of the object of this concept, without adding anything to the concept itself. It concerns, as Kant indicates, the relation of the thing to the whole condition of my thought—namely, that a posteriori knowledge of that object is also possible, that is, situated within the context of all experience. In a passage that has become famous, Kant gives an example of the relation between being and being-something that obtains here: the concept of a hundred actual taler cannot contain the slightest bit more than a hundred possible ones. Anyone who infers from just the concept of the highest being that such a being exists produces as little real insight as a businessman increases his real buying power by adding a few zeros to his account books in order to improve his finances. We really must give up these bankrupt frauds of speculative reason. Existence can never be "cobbled out" of ideas—that would be nothing but unnatural Scholasticism.

This is Kant's critique of the ontological proof. Kant is not the first to have rejected Anselm's proof. At the beginning, it generally received only limited acceptance. Thomas too rejected it. Kant's critique is more decisive than all its predecessors, however, to the extent that Kant intended to expose the pretext of dialectical argument as the real kernel of all other speculative proofs of God as well, so that with the one proof all others fall too. Before we enter into a clarification of the problems involved here, we should quickly follow Kant's critique to its conclusion.

If the ontological argument about the highest "reality" (*Sachhaltigkeit*) implies the necessity of its being, the cosmological proof of the unconditional necessity of a being, summarized above, implies its unlimited reality. This proof therefore claims that it proceeds on the basis of experience—or, better, the object of all possible experience, the real world. If something exists, then an absolutely necessary being must exist (because, that is, every contingency must have its cause, and the series of causes must begin with an absolutely necessary cause). Now Kant shows that to conclude the existence of the necessary being from the being that is most real of all fundamentally already presupposes the opposite, ontological conclusion. (Logically speaking, it is a *conversio per accidens* that amounts to a *conversio simplex*.) According to Kant, this alone suffices to expose this argument's claim to probative value, quite aside from any critical objections to applying the concept of causation to a necessary being situated beyond experience. This application leads to thickening even more the dialectical appearance of the argument, falsely making it seem an independent proof of its own. The idea of one per se necessary being already involves the nonsense of the ontological argument: its existence is supposed to be already implied in its concept. Thus, in the transcendental ideal of an absolutely necessary being, Kant sees not an objective founding principle that pertains to the things themselves, but only a subjective principle of reason, a regulative idea. Merely to bring systematic unity to our knowledge—certainly a justifiable demand of reason—one must assume an initial necessary ground. It is, then, a mere "as if," which (taken "hypostatically") strengthens the plausibility of the ontological argument.

Finally, the physico-theological argument. From the particular constitution of the world—its order, purposefulness, and beauty—it derives a first, original cause in which all possible perfections are united, an inference viewed with respect now as then, and thus singled out by Kant as well. Kant's point of departure seems indeed natural and unobjectionable. The purposefulness of nature—a supposition that proves again and again to be a fruitful leitmotiv of research—is supposed to imply a corresponding cause of the greatest power and perfection. If we look more closely, however, it appears that experience implies only an indeterminate, relatively great cause, never an absolute totality. It would probably have to be an understanding greater than that of any human being, but never the greatest possible understanding, which is called wisdom. To draw this conclusion would itself presuppose that we possess omniscience (of natural causes). Here too, Kant shows, a being necessary in itself cannot be derived from contingency. This means, though, that the supposed empirical proof of God is truly empirical only as long as it never arrives at its real object, but instead stays within the limits of empirical applicability. If, on the other hand it posits a divine understanding, not merely an expanded human one, it becomes a transcendental proof in the style of the cosmological and ontological proofs already criticized. The ontological proof, then, is the only possible speculative proof of God—the very one that proved to be dialectical.

Transcendental theology is thereby shown to be useful only for negative, not dogmatic purposes—that is, it is of use only on the presupposition that the concept of the highest being can be safely applied in some other, perhaps practical situations. Specifically, it can assist in defining the concept of God correctly and in defending against dogmatic objections. This is, in fact, Kant's opinion. There is only one moral proof of God, and that is grounded on the ineluctable demands of practical reason, after balancing duty and happiness. This conclusion too is merely postulative in character. But, unlike the others above, its end is not an improved knowledge of being; rather, it follows directly from the categorical character of morality and thus is oriented toward practice. Only by presupposing this ethico-theological proof based on ultimate purpose can *the speculative proof*—in particular the physico-theological—belatedly come into its own.

For Kant, this proof of God from a practical point of view undoubtedly represents the deepest and most characteristic impulse of his critical philosophy. He himself said that he destroyed the claim of knowledge in order to make room for faith. Doubtless, too, Kant can hardly be accused of misunderstanding reason's natural disposition to view itself as a theoretical god. But the yardstick of certain conviction that guided him, and that reached its apex in the exemplary form of practical certainty about duty and freedom, subjected speculative reason to critique. This critique denied theoretical knowledge of God's existence, because it limited theoretical reason generally to the arena of possible experience. Only this negative aspect of critique, not the positive practical aspect, has persisted in the general consciousness—especially thanks to the neo-Kantian orientation of philosophy of the sciences. The Kantian notion of duty had its effect then and now. The theology postulated on it, however, sank into oblivion just as much as the proofs of God that Kant criticized.

If we now turn to the systematic philosophical problems in Kant's polemic that have retained some life and survived history, we can prepare ourselves by recalling what Hegel said about reestablishing the weight of this proof beyond its sense: "[it] is obviously inappropriate—as if knowing and being convinced of it could of themselves essentially produce faith and the conviction that God exists." Hegel compares this assertion with the statement that we cannot eat before studying the food chemically, botanically, and zoologically. Philosophy consists, rather, in rethinking religious ideas in which thought is already involved. The proofs of God, thus conceived, are ways of raising thought beyond the sensible to God, where they constitute a new mode of devotion. This means, however, that they are not so much proofs of God's existence as ways of thoughtfully knowing God through the character of his necessity, wisdom, and so on. The question about God's existence, then, is precisely one that cannot be erected on a proof of existence that inquires into an existent unknown in itself that has the same mode of being as an object of experience. Instead, it must ask what God is supposed to be like. Thus far Hegel.

Let us inspect Kant's proofs and his critique of them in terms of this way of putting the question. What is the philosophical kernel of the ontological argument that underlies all the others? We can say with Scheler that the distinction between being-something and being-that, the yawning abyss between thinkable possibilities and reality, Kant's great theme, the dependence of rational cognition upon experience, clearly implies the inconceivability of reality. In the realm of thought, everything is easily accomplished, limitlessly replaceable, the future as much at our command as the past; thus too, for thought, all reality becomes subject to the fluid possibility of its desires; and it thinks of itself as the lord of everything real. This means, however, that in self-consciousness, where the thinker produces himself from everything that he thinks, he inquires about everything, even about the possibility of the nothing. Why is there a world at all, and why am "I" at all? Why isn't there nothing?—It is this abyss of the nothing, the horrible experience of the contingency of being that reason traces back to what is necessary in itself—that is, God. Or, as Scheler says, when he assigns a key position to this cosmological proof based on the world's contingency: consciousness of God is equiprimordial with consciousness of self and the world. Proof of God can be based neither on the world nor on the "I am," because consciousness of world, self, and God form an indissoluble unity (admittedly, only the concept of God as a necessary world ground).

Let us now consider Kant's critique of the cosmological proof. Kant discerns that the weakness of the ontological argument consists in the difficulty inherent in the concept of an unconditional necessity. Reason recognizes as absolutely necessary only what is necessary by reason of its concept.

> Unconditioned necessity, which we so indispensably require as the last bearer of all things, is for human reason the veritable abyss. Eternity itself, in all its terrible sublimity, as depicted by a Haller, is

far from making the same overwhelming impression on the mind; for it only *measures* the duration of things, it does not *support* them. We cannot put aside, and yet also cannot endure the thought, that a being, which we represent to ourselves as supreme amongst all possible beings, should, as it were, say to itself: "I am from eternity to eternity, and outside me there is nothing save what is through my will, *but whence then am I?*" All support here fails us; and the *greatest* perfection, no less than the *least* perfection, is insubstantial and baseless for the merely speculative reason, which makes not the least effort to retain either the one or the other, and feels indeed no loss in allowing them to vanish entirely. (B641; trans. Kemp Smith)

We see that Kant is radical. The necessary in itself is a nonconcept. Everything that we posit conceptually can be nonexistent as well. From concepts, being does not follow. This cleft is not to be closed up.

For us, however, this consideration concerning the ontological argument has a much more serious aspect than it did for Kant, because his critique validated empirical knowledge of nature as well as practical reason's faith in God (along with the unconditional character of moral law). For us the nihilism of speculative reason came to be total nihilism with Nietzsche. It is not just that God is dead: self and world too "are" no more; instead, what is is solely and exclusively the will to power, for which truth is a value that serves to preserve power. The world, moreover, is an interpretation necessitated by life. The "I" is likewise not an immediate given, but a perspectivized silhouette projected by the will to power. This radical nihilism must be viewed as the destructive consequence of German Idealism if we want to discern how the question of God is alive and contemporary.

The first person to have taken this Idealistic principle to its ultimate metaphysical conclusion, we recall, was Leibniz. As a radical Cartesian, he took the mode of being of the *res cogitans* as the basis of the genuinely metaphysical world view. The monad is a "thinking" unity. Within the prestabilized harmony that is the genial hypothesis of his system, the plurality of monads—each of which has its own world and its own perspective on a being that for us is not thinkable at all apart from some perspective—is bound up in unity. As body and soul correspond in preestablished parallelism, so too, in strictly predetermined ways, I and Thou correspond in our perceptions of the world as in our being for each other; so that in the most complete, windowless isolation of each monad, the commonality of the world and a whole world of community become possible. God has set all clocks so exactly that they all sound the same hour of being. This is how Leibniz sees it. But what preserves the unity of the world, the commonality and community for the modern plurality of wills to power, when there is no being at all, only the power struggle among interpretations? The common world that we all inhabit in our naive credulity and consider to be the true one is supposed to be only a form of the will to power. It is as little true as false—just as little as there is a good or an evil. The question is: In this situation, is the question of God still alive? Is it wrapped up in the question concerning true being— being that would be accessible for a true, cognitive knowledge that did not just project life perspectives, as is the multiplicity of monads for the divine creator of their harmony? Nietzsche did not deny the problem for thought that is involved here. His mad god Dionysus is conceived thus. He is supposed as having impressed the stamp of "being" on "becoming" itself.

We understand Nietzsche's nihilism as the logical sharpening of modern subjectivism. Basing philosophy on the subjectivity of self-consciousness ends in the dynamic of life forces that undergird and form consciousness itself. Idealism ends in the will to power.

It seems to me, then, that a general philosophical problem is involved here, and that the question of God, taken as meaningful, includes the problem of supraindividual being. Ever since the nominalist interpretation of Aristotle in the Middle Ages, what really exists is the single individual. All generalities—type and kind, idea and law—are merely secondary, constructs of synthetic reason, which unifies all. This fundamental presupposition still underlies Kant's critique of the ontological argument as well. From the idea of a perfect being, its existence follows just as little as from any other idea; existence follows from some experiential encounter, and from that alone. An "idea" such as maximal "realitas," however, can never be encountered in the context of experience. The question arises, though, whether the nominalist presupposition of Kant's critique is appropriate.

It cannot be doubted that Kant's critique of the ontological argument and his rejection of all speculative proofs of God do justice to neither Anselm nor his medieval opponents. In fact, Anselm himself had already raised this point in rebutting Gaunilo's critique of his argument: the crux of that argument was no arbitrary conclusion, inferring the reality from the concept, but instead a conclusion that holds only in the one unique case of a greatness than which nothing greater is thinkable—and clearly this holds because what is so thought is thereby elevated by faith beyond comparison with other thinkable or existing things. Only thus can we understand the power of the concept of maximal reality that carries its existence with it. Kant, by contrast, equates the idea of God with anything that can be thought in a representation—hence his example of the 100 talers. This equation, however, rests on reducing the concept of being to being-that and reducing the "experience" corresponding to it to what is individuated in the pure form of intuition and to what can be determined by "science" and its way of measuring. The medieval proof of God, just the opposite, depends on a "realist" conception of being that distinguishes various grades and levels within being itself: an order of creation that involves ascribing to each being a higher mode of being at the same time.

We cannot go along with this. Yet for us too the question arises whether we can do justice to our experiences and the philosophical tasks they set for us, if we view verifiability through observation as the real essence of being and thereby conceive of natural science as the sole real form of experience and of scientific knowledge. That the being of an organism is more than the mere sum of the individual physical and chemical processes accessible to scientific experimental observation; that we must do research on plants in other ways than on animals, because they really are different; that along with physics in the broadest sense there is an originary scientific experience of forms and ways of conducting oneself—all these point to the truths of medieval "realism," as do the phenomena of so-called objective mind: namely, language, custom, state, art, and so forth. On the nominalist presuppositions of seventeenth- and eighteenth-century science, understanding these formations of objective spirit meets with difficulties. That they exist only in single individuals (their "bearers")—rather than individuals existing only insofar as state, custom, and language with their being-forming power manifest themselves in them—or that the universal of the state derives its validity from the unconstrained rights of individuals, these are not merely the mistaken interpretations of the real nature of being. These are modes of modern human beings' comportment toward being, on which much depends because they depend on the view of being. The universalization of nominalistically grounded science certainly depends on the indubitability of the knowledge produced by it. But that what is known in this way does not exhaust what truly is worth knowing is an experience just as compelling as an experience of the limits of what is supposedly free, the scientifically validated ability to control nature and the heart. So it is precisely the experience of the limits of freedom—of ability and of knowledge, the fact that all of us are determined by supraindividual powers, which brings into question the modern presupposition that the individual, and preeminently the individual person, represents the ens realissimum of all beings. History, fate, death, the experience of the finitude of the infinitely inquiring spirit—these boundary experiences are the modern analogues of the experience on which Kant's critique is based. Kant was able to construct a moral metaphysics upon his critique of speculative metaphysics. In similar fashion, Jaspers has recently grounded metaphysics on fundamental experiences of human "existence." Since modern subjectivism is radically— that is, morally—nihilistic, and the person must view his freedom as unbounded, he experiences his own boundaries, so that all his presuppositions (and not just the speculative ones) are shaken. In this way he is again brought nearer to the "realistic" conception of being. In our situation, the meaning of ancient, thoroughly self-evident "realism" is that the experience of supraindividual ontological realities is not to be won from the empirical pride that nominalistically levels everything out. Rather, the Greeks discerned in the being of the universal, the common and binding, the higher reality of being. As Euripides simply put it: "To embrace one's friends—that is god" (ἀσπάζειν τοὺς φίλους θεός).

Such "humanistic" experience of the divine is perhaps most compellingly expressed in Hölderlin's poetry. That it does not do justice to the Christian conception of God cannot be ignored. Yet, when modern philosophy begins to entrust itself to the ancient path of thought, perhaps thinkers will learn once again to discern the ancient content of the concept of God.

2

On the Possibility of a
Philosophical Ethics (1963)

It is by no means evident that a "philosophical" ethics, a moral philosophy, is something different from a "practical" ethics — that is, from constructing a list of values to which the agent appeals, and from the knowledge of how to apply them that guides his appeal to this list of values in practice. In antiquity, by contrast, it was obvious that the philosophical pragmatics which, since Aristotle, has been called "ethics" was itself a "practical" knowledge. Aristotle gave expression to what was basically already implicit in the Socratic and Platonic doctrine about the knowledge of virtue — namely, that we do not just want to know what virtue is, but to know it in order to become good. For Aristotle, too, this is what is special about ethical pragmatics; yet it belongs to the ancient concept of knowledge generally that the transition to *praxis* is inherent in it: knowledge (*Wissenschaft*) is not an aggregate of anonymous truths, but a human comportment (ἕξις τοῦ ἀληθεύειν). Even "theoria" does not stand in absolute opposition to praxis, but is itself the highest praxis, one of the highest modes of human being. As Aristotle recognized, this obtains for the highest knowledge, the knowledge of first things, philosophical knowledge, even if there is a tension between epistemic knowledge (ἐπιστήμη, τέχνη) and experiential knowledge, so that the experienced practitioner is oftentimes superior to the "learned" expert. This non-dichotomy is wholly the case in the ethical sphere, where there can be no such tension between theory and practice, because there are no experts at applying it.

On the other hand, there is the modern concept of rational "theory," defined from the ground up by reference to its practical application—and that means by opposition to its practical application. In certain ways, there has always been an opposition between books and life. But it is only with the dawning of modernity, especially in the age of humanism, when the Hellenistic ideal of *sapientia* was revitalized and combined with the critique of Scholasticism, of *doctrina*, that it emerged fully into consciousness. Nicholas of Cusa put his perspicuous doctrines in the mouth of the layman, the "idiota," who sees more perspicuously than the "orator" and "philosophus" with whom he is speaking. It is with the rise of modern science that the opposition as such becomes fully fixed and at the same time the concept of theory acquires a new profile. Theory now means an explanation of the multiplicity of appearances, enabling them to be mastered. Understood as a tool, it ceases being a properly human action, and in contrast to such, it claims to be more than a relative truth.

Such a conception of theory, one that has become pretty much patent to us all, leads to a nearly indissoluble *aporia* when applied to moral phenomena. It seems to be unavoidably tied to an optimistic progressivism, since the course of scientific research aims at producing ever newer, ever more exact theoretical knowledge. Applied to the moral world, however, it becomes an absurd belief in moral progress. Here Rousseau's critique of the Enlightenment has pronounced a veto that cannot be overridden. Kant himself acknowledged as much: "Rousseau set me straight." The *Foundation of the Metaphysics of Morals* allows no doubt that moral philosophy is "the universal knowledge of moral reason"—that is, the consciousness of an obligation to do what a simple heart and level head says is right can never be superseded. Nevertheless, moral philosophical reflections, according to Kant, do not present themselves as mere theory. Rather, so forceful is Kant's moral reproof of the Enlightenment's pride in reasoning that he teaches the necessity of the transition to moral philosophy; thus it has basically remained the case that moral philosophy can never completely disavow its own moral relevance. Max Scheler, founder of the material ethics of value, was taken to task by one of his students because he explained the system of values and its normative power so clearly, yet followed it so little in the conduct of his life. Scheler replied, "Does the signpost go in the direction it points?" This is obviously unsatisfactory. Tellingly, Nicolai Hartmann, who systematically elaborated Scheler's ethical conception, could not avoid ascribing to philosophy of value a moral significance as well. It has, he suggests, a maieutic function for consciousness of moral value; that is, it affords an ever richer explication of the moral, in that it reveals forgotten or unrecognized values. This is all that is left of the old expectation that the philosopher is held to: namely, that in the midst of moral perplexity and confusion, he should not merely pursue his passion for theory, but rather ground ethics anew—that is, construct new tables of binding values. Admittedly, it may well be that Heidegger is right when he begins his "Letter on Humanism" with the answer to the question "When will you write an ethics?": "For a long time we have not considered the essence of action decisively enough."

In fact, it does appear that there is an inescapable difficulty in the idea of moral philosophy itself. It was first brought to our awareness in Kierkegaard's critique of Hegel and of the Christian Church. Kierkegaard showed that all "knowing at a distance" is insufficient for the fundamental moral and religious situation of humankind. Just as the meaning of the Christian revelation is to be experienced and accepted as "contemporaneous" (*gleichzeitig*), so also ethical choice is no matter of theoretical knowledge, but rather the brightness, sharpness, and pressure of conscience. All knowing at a distance threatens to veil or to weaken the demand that is implicit in the situation of moral choice. In our century, we recall, the critique of neo-Kantian idealism coming from theological and philosophical quarters, under Kierkegaard's influence, brought the fundamental questionability of ethics to our cognizance. Insofar as ethics is understood as knowledge of the universal, it is implicated in the moral questionableness associated with the concept of the universal law. It is to the epistle to the Romans that one turns first of all. The idea that sin comes from the law is understood not in the sense that the forbidden is tempting and thus encourages sin, but rather in the sense that keeping the law is precisely what leads to the real sin—which is not just the occasional transgression of the law but that *superbia* that prevents those obeying the law from obeying the commandment to love. It is not the priest and the Levite but the Samaritan who accepts and fulfills the requirement of love deriving from the situation. From the philosophical side, too, it is by beginning with the concept of the situation that the questionableness of the idea of ethics is sharpened to the utmost extreme—for example, by Eberhard Grisebach, the philosophical friend of Gogarten.

In this context philosophical ethics does indeed seem to be in an insoluble dilemma. The reflexive generality which is necessarily its philosophical metier entangles it in the questionableness of law-based ethics. How can it do justice to the concreteness with which conscience, sensitivity to equity, and loving reconciliation are answerable to the situation?

There are, I believe, only two ways to extricate philosophical ethics from this dilemma. One is that of ethical formalism, stemming from Kant; the other is the way of Aristotle. Neither can do justice to the possibility of philosophical ethics per se, but both can do so for their parts of it.

Kant inquires into the sole kind of obligation which, because of its unconditional universality, will suffice for the concept of ethics. He discerned that the only mode of ethical obligation capable of serving as an ethics is the unconditional duty that obliges the agent against interest and inclination. His categorical imperative is to be understood as the first principle of every moral system precisely because it does nothing but present the form of obligation implicit in Ought—that is, the unconditional quality of the moral law. If there is a moral good will, then it must be adequate to this form. That such unconditional good will does exist, that the categorical imperative is therefore capable of really determining our will, is not of course demonstrated through this knowledge of the universal "form" of the moral. To this question the metaphysician Kant gives a prepared answer in the *Critique of Pure Reason*. To be sure, every factical determination of the will belonging to the phenomenal realm is subject to the basic principles of experience, and among them an unconditionally good action is certainly never to be met with. But the self-limitation of pure reason has shown that outside the phenomenal order, where there is only the relation of cause and effect, there exists yet another intelligible order, to which we belong not as sensible but as rational beings and within which the standpoint of freedom, the self-legislation of reason, can be rightly understood. That we "ought" is something we know with practical reason's unconditional certainty, which is not contradicted by theoretical understanding. Freedom is theoretically not impossible, and it is practically necessary.

On this basis, Kant derives an answer to the question, why moral-philosophical deliberation is necessary without moral philosophy's thereby transcending the law-creating simplicity of the simple consciousness of duty. Specifically, Kant says, "Innocence is a wonderful thing, and conversely it is really too bad that it cannot be preserved but is easily seduced."[1] The innocence of the simple heart that knows its duty unerringly consists not so much in not being led astray by overpowering inclinations; rather, the heart's innocence manifests itself in the fact that whenever it deviates from the path of justice, which always happens except in a completely "holy will," it nevertheless still unerringly recognizes what is unjust; it absolutely resists not overpowering inclinations, but only the errors caused by reason itself. That is to say, among affective promptings, practical reason unfolds a specific dialectic through which it knows how to attenuate a given duty's power to obligate. It makes use of what I would like to call the "dialectic of the exception." It does not contest the validity of the moral law but, rather, tries to underscore the exceptional nature of the situation in which the agent finds himself—in the sense that whatever the validity of the law, exceptions are nevertheless justified under certain circumstances. Moral-philosophical reflection can come to the aid of moral reason threatened by such temptations. It needs such aid all the more when moral-philosophical reflection in its "universal" form itself abets this temptation. In that Kant's *Foundation* discerns the essence of moral obligation in its being without exception—that is the meaning of the categorical imperative—it establishes the purity of the decisions of moral reason.

The meaning of Kantian formalism, then, consists in certifying the purity of such decisions against all the turbidity coming from the viewpoint of inclination and interest—in the naive consciousness as in the philosophical. To that extent Kant's rigor—where the only cultivated will that possesses moral value is the one that acts purely out of duty and against all inclination—has a clear methodological significance. In Hegel's terms, what emerges here is the form of reason that tests laws.[2]

Here, however, the question arises how such testing occurs

at all, given human reason's dependence on experience and its deep-rooted "inclination to evil." As Gerhard Krüger has pointed out,[3] Kant's moral philosophical reflections presuppose recognition of the moral law. The formulas which, as types, lie ready at hand to the judgment—for example, that of natural law or that of purpose in itself—are so unreal that in themselves they never have any persuasive power. Recall the person who commits suicide, for example: Kant says that if such a person is still sufficiently in possession of his reason that he can test his decision to commit suicide against the model of such a formula, then he will arrive at the insight that his decision is untenable. That, however, is obviously a mere construction. It is precisely the person haunted by thoughts of suicide who lacks that much reason. Though the ethical impermissibility of suicide could be perceived in this way, the very fact that a person is prepared to think things through (which is the only way someone would come to this insight in the first place) presupposes, even more, a motivation for examining one's conscience. Where does that come from? Kant's formula seems to be of merely methodological relevance to reflection, since it teaches us to exclude all the muddiness of "inclination."

Kant's rigor has still another moral meaning beyond the methodological contrast between duty and inclination. What Kant has in mind is the following: extreme cases—in which, against all inclination, a person takes to heart his true duty—let him, as it were, internalize the power of his moral reason and thus build a firm foundation for his character. He comes to an awareness of the moral laws that guide his life. He is formed by the exceptional situation in which he has to pass the test that he, as it were, sets himself (see, for example, the doctrine of method of the pure practical reason in the *Critique of Practical Reason*).

On the other hand, we need to ask what defines such exceptional situations wherein the contrast between duty and inclination is sharpened to the point of decision. It is not just any situation that can be elevated into an occasion for preserving genuine moral resoluteness and testing one's conscience. Hegel's well-known critique of the immorality of the Ought— because Ought already presupposes a contradiction to Want and thus also presupposes the evil will—comes in here. Isn't he right when he discerns the essence of ethics not in the self-necessity of an imperative ethics, but in the ethos—that is, in the substantiality of the moral order that has its embodiment in the great objectivities of family, society, and state? The truth of moral consciousness lies not merely in the scrupulousness with which it continually tries to become tortuously conscious of impure motives and inclinations. Of course there are occasions of conflict when such moral self-examination takes place. Conscience, however, has no permanent *habitus;* instead, it is something by which we are struck, by which we are awakened.[4] And how? Isn't there such a thing as a "broad" conscience? It can hardly be denied that the wakefulness of conscience depends upon orders of substance in which one always already lives. The autonomous moral reason, therefore, assuredly has the character of intelligible self-determination; but that does not exclude the fact that all human action and decision are conditioned by experience. At the very least, in judging others—and this too belongs to the moral sphere—one cannot ignore their being conditioned. What one can demand of others (morally and not just legally) is not the same as what one can demand of oneself. Indeed, recognizing human conditionedness (in a charitable judgment) is quite compatible with the sublime unconditionality of the moral law. It is indicative of Kant's reflective thematic that he is not interested in the difference between a judgment of conscience about oneself and one's moral judgment of another. For this reason, Kant's way out of our question about the moral meaning of moral philosophy seems to me finally unsatisfactory. We can concede, of course, that no one is spared situations of moral conflict, and to that extent the temptation to consider oneself an exception is a universal human situation. From this does it not follow, however, that the transition to a metaphysics of morals is necessary for everyone? Kant does indeed draw this conclusion. His grounding of the moral is meant to bring the secret metaphysics of every ethics to greater clarity —but also to give it greater moral fixity. But is such a conclusion tolerable? Has not Kant sublated Rousseau in himself again?

So it seems to me that another kind of testing is valuable: a moral-philosophical deliberation that chooses to orient itself not via the exceptional case of conflict, but the regular case of following a moral custom. We might consider the objection to an ethics of the pure Ought and orientation to the reflective form of moral consciousness that has been raised in our century especially by the ethics of material value that Max Scheler and Nicolai Hartmann developed. It has consciously situated itself in opposition to Kant's formalism. Though in Scheler's work it has immoderately and unjustly misinterpreted the rational character of Kant's formalism of duty; nevertheless, it has also performed the incontestably positive function of making the object of moral-philosophical analysis the substantive content of morality, not just the conflict between Ought and Want. The concept of value that is raised here to systematic significance is meant to break open the narrow focus on the concept of duty— that is, the focus on the mere goals of effort and the norms of the Ought. There are morally valuable things that cannot be made the object of effort and cannot be demanded. There is, for example, no duty to love. Kant's fatal revision of the Christian commandment that we love one another into a duty to perform tasks of practical charity speaks volumes in this respect. Love, even viewed in moral terms, is something nobler than the charitable acts that duty requires. Relying on the phenomenological theory that the laws of essence and of the a priori generally are immediately evident, Scheler grounded an a priori system of value upon the immediacy of the a priori consciousness of value. This not only comprehended the proper goals for which moral will strives; it also delved down into the vital sphere and the sphere of utilitarian values, as well as reaching up into the sphere of the holy. Such an ethics really comprehends the substantive contents of morality, not just the reflective phenomenon of the reason that tests laws.

Even if such an ethics of value expressly includes the concept of ethos and the changing forms it takes, however, it cannot escape the inherent consequence of its methodological claim to intuit a priori systems of value. This is especially clear in the case of Nicolai Hartmann, who conceives of the a priori hierarchy of values not as a self-enclosed system whose highest value is the holy, but rather as an open region of values, a boundless object of human experience and at the same time the subject of unbounded research. The progress of research discovers ever finer structures and relationships of value and thus justifies being itself dominated by value-blindness. Ultimately this must imply, however, that research in ethics as value itself requires and refines ethical consciousness. For that reason, moral philosophy certainly cannot teach with authority—that is, posit new values; but it can develop moral consciousness in such a way that it discovers these values in itself. As Nicolai Hartmann says, moral philosophy therefore has a maieutic function.

Such a theory founders, however, on the necessity (rightly recognized by Scheler) that every morality is a concrete ethical form. If it is made the guiding idea of an ethics of material value, the idea of an infinite refinement of value consciousness must quite unavoidably also imply and ground its own ethos—

indeed, one to which other ethical forms can be juxtaposed. One thinks, for example, of what is specially emphasized by Hartmann: the value of abundance violated by "passing by" (Nietzsche). The ethics of value has an immanent and ineluctable limitation: it itself constructs an ethics which contradicts the methodological claim to be aprioristic research in value. This methodological claim can be fulfilled by no human (and that ultimately means by no historically applicable) moral system at all. What the fundamental idea of an a priori value system essentially calls for is an infinite subject. Thus an ethics of material value, while including the substantive content of morality, unlike Kantian formalism, does not find the way out that we are searching for. Moral philosophy and the immediacy of value consciousness remain split asunder.

Let us, then, orient ourselves instead on Aristotle,[5] who has no concept of value, but rather "virtues" and "goods," and who became the founder of philosophical ethics by correcting the "intellectualism" of Socrates and Plato without sacrificing its essential insights. The concept of ethos with which he began makes precisely this explicit: "virtue" does not consist merely in knowledge, for the possibility of knowing depends, to the contrary, on what a person is like, and the being of each one is formed beforehand through his or her education and way of life. Perhaps Aristotle's view is focused more intensely on the conditionedness of our moral being, on the dependence of the individual decision on the practical and social determinants of the time, and less on the unconditionality that pertains to the ethical phenomenon. It was precisely the latter that Kant successfully worked out in its purity, the same purity possessed by its wonderful complement in antiquity: namely, Plato's inquiry into "justice as such," which undergirds his whole projected state. Aristotle succeeded, however, in rendering the nature of moral knowledge so clear that (under the concept of "choice of") it covers just as much the subjectivity that judges in the case of conflict as the substance of law and custom which determines its moral knowledge and its particular choices. His analysis of *phronesis* recognizes that moral knowledge is a way of moral being itself, which therefore cannot be prescinded from the whole concretion of what he calls ethos. Moral knowledge discerns what needs to be done, what a situation requires; and it discerns what is doable on the basis of a conviction that the concrete situation is related to what is considered right and proper in general. It has, therefore, the structure of a conclusion in which one premise is the general knowledge of what is right, as that is adumbrated in conceptualized ethical values. At the same time, what is happening here is not mere subsumption, merely a successful judgment, for whether such deliberation is undertaken without deviation depends on the being of the person. People who are overwhelmed with emotion get lost in these deliberations — that is, in the process of orienting themselves on the basis of moral conviction. They are, as it were, momentarily benighted.[6] Aristotle explains this by reference to the intoxicated: the unaccountability of someone who is drunk involves no moral unaccountability, for he had it in his power to drink moderately.

The crux of Aristotle's philosophical ethics, then, lies in the mediation between logos and ethos, between the subjectivity of knowing and the substance of being. Moral knowledge does not climax in courage, justice, and so on, but rather in the concrete application that determines in the light of such knowledge what should be done here and now. It has been rightly brought to our attention that Aristotle's last pronouncement concerning what is right consists in the vague phrase "as befits it" (ὡς δεῖ). It is not the grand conceptualizations of an ethics based on heroic exemplars and its "table of values" that are the real content of Aristotelian ethics; it is, rather, the undeluded and undeceptive concrete moral consciousness (ὡς ὁ λόγος ὀρθὸς λέγει) that finds expression in such unmeaning and all-inclusive concepts as what is "fitting," what is "proper," what is "good and right." It is a mistake for people to take Aristotle's emphasis on this universal formula for concretization and turn it into a pseudo-objectivity, seeing a special "value of the situation" written therein (N. Hartmann). Quite the contrary, this is precisely the meaning of the doctrine of the "mean" that Aristotle develops: that all conceptual definitions of traditional virtues possess at best a schematic or typical correctness, which is produced from the *legomena*. This means, however, that philosophical ethics finds itself in the same situation as everyone else. That which we consider right, which we affirm or reject, follows from our general ideas about what is good and right. It achieves its real determinacy, nevertheless, only from the concrete reality of the case. This is not a case of applying a universal rule. Just the opposite: it is the real thing we are concerned with, and for this the generic forms of the virtues and the structure of the "mean" that Aristotle points out in them offer only a vague schema. Thus it is phronesis—the virtue enabling one to hit upon the mean and achieve the concretization—which shows that something can be done (πρακτὸν ἀγαθόν), not some faculty special to philosophers. On the contrary, those who deliberate on what is good and right in general see themselves as referring to this practical logos just like everyone else who has to put their ideas of what is good and right into action. Aristotle explicitly refers to the mistake of people who resort to theorizing and, instead of doing what is right, just philosophize about it.[7]

Thus it is certainly not true, as sometimes appears to be the case in Aristotle, that phronesis has to do with finding the right means to a pregiven end. This concrete moral deliberation defines the "purpose" for the first time by making it concrete— that is, by defining what "should be done" (as πρακτὸν ἀγαθόν).

Kant is certainly right to view the ideal of happiness as an ideal more of imagination than of reason, and to that extent it is completely right to say that no determinate content can be specified for the determination of our will that would be universally binding and capable of being defended as a moral law by our reason. Yet we need to ask whether the autonomy of practical reason—defending the unconditional nature of our duty against the persuasions of our inclinations—represents nothing more than a check upon our caprice, and is not determined by the entirety of our moral being, which whole (permeated by the patency of what is right) comports itself practically in each case whenever it chooses what to do. (By *hexis* is meant not a capacity for being this or that, like knowing and understanding are, but instead an ontological category like nature, a "thus and not otherwise.")

What should be done: this is admittedly not just what is right, but also what is useful, purposeful, and in that sense "right." The interpenetration of these two senses of "right" in humankind's practical conduct is clearly what for Aristotle constitutes the humanly good. Obviously those who act in a morally right manner do not comport themselves in the same way as does a craftsman who knows his business (τέχνη). Moral action is not right by reason of the fact that what is thereby brought into existence is right; rather, its rightness lies primarily in ourselves, in the "how" of our conduct, in the manner in which the person who "is right" does it (the σπουδαῖος ἀνήρ). It is also true, on the other hand, that in our moral conduct, which depends so much more on our being than on our explicit consciousness (εἰδώς), we ourselves are drawn forth as well—as we are (and not as we know ourselves). Yet, insofar as the whole of our being depends upon capabilities, possibilities, and circumstances that are not simply given over into our hands, *eupraxia*, the end of our conduct, and *eudaimonia*, at which we are aiming and for which we are striving, comprehend more than we ourselves are. Our actions are situated within the horizon of the polis, and thus our choice of what is to be done spreads out into the whole of our external social being.

Ethics proves to be a part of politics. For the concretization of our selves—whose circumference is sketched out in the forms of virtue and their being ordered toward the highest and most desirable form of life—reaches far into what is common to us all, which the Greeks named the polis, and to the true form of which everyone is at all times answerable. Only now does it become intelligible that friendship is a central object of Aristotle's pragmatics—not as "love of friends," but as that mean between virtues and goods which is only *met'aretes*. Without it—and it is always a precarious possession—a full life is unimaginable.[8]

Thus Aristotle does not emphasize the sublime unconditionality in moral decision making that Plato and Kant demand. Of course, Aristotle too knows that moral conduct does not simply pursue arbitrarily chosen purposes, but rather chooses something for its own sake, because it is "well" (*schön*). But on the whole it is always the task of a being that is limited and conditioned in multifaceted respects to see and master this. Even the noblest ideal of human existence, pure contemplation—toward which the whole structure of Aristotle's ethics, like Plato's,[9] always gravitates—remains tied to governing well the life of action on which that very ideal itself depends.

It is in this way, however, that the sense for the multiply conditioned, which constitutes Aristotle's speculative genius, becomes fruitful for moral philosophy; for here and here alone emerges an answer to the question that has been plaguing us: namely, how a philosophical ethics, a human doctrine of the human, is possible without requiring a superhuman self-transcendence.

The moral-philosophical deliberation that is implicit in the practice of philosophical ethics is not a theory that must be made practically applicable. It is not at all a knowing in general, a knowing at a distance, which would in fact conceal what the concrete situation calls for, like the priest and the Levite's sense of fidelity to the law by contrast to the Good Samaritan's. The universal, the generic, that can be expressed only in a philosophical inquiry dedicated to conceptual universality is in fact not essentially different from what guides the usual, completely untheoretical sense of norms present in every deliberation on moral practice. Most important, it is not different from this untheoretical deliberation, in that it includes the same task of application to given circumstances that obtains for all moral knowledge, for the individual as well as the statesman who acts on behalf of all. It is not just phronesis, moral knowledge that guides concrete action, that has a moral being, an *arete* (it is ἕξις, admittedly a ἕξις τοῦ ἀληθεύειν). The philosophical practice of ethics too has a moral relevance, and that is not a hybrid "academic" claim divorced from "life," but rather a necessary consequence of the fact that it is always situated within circumstances that condition it. It is not something for anyone and everyone, but only for those whose education in society and state has brought their own being to a point of such maturity that they are capable of recognizing general rules of thumb in concrete perplexities and putting them into practice. The audience of Aristotle's lectures on ethics themselves needed to get beyond the temptation only to philosophize and to abstract themselves from the claims of the situation. To keep this danger always before one's eyes: this, I think, is why Aristotle is still not outmoded. Like Kant with his "formalism," Aristotle too distanced himself from all false claims incident to the idea of a philosophical ethics. Whereas Kant destroyed the moral-philosophical rationalizations of the Enlightenment and its blind pride in reason by releasing unconditional practical reason from all the conditionedness of human nature and presenting it in transcendental purity, Aristotle, by contrast, placed the conditionedness of human life at the center and singled out concretizing the universal, by applying it to the given situation, as the central task of philosophical ethics and moral conduct alike. We owe Kant our unending thanks for disclosing the consequential impurity of moral reasonings, that "disgusting mishmash" of moral and practical motives which the "practical worldly wisdom" of the Enlightenment validated as a higher form of morality. From this madness Kant helped us recover. There is another aspect of things, however, which makes it necessary for us to take into account the conditionedness of all human being and also, therefore, of our use of reason. Above all, it is the aspect of education that makes manifest humankind's essential conditionedness. Kant too knows about this, but the limits of his truth become visible in the way he knows about it. Kant shows very impressively how much power the ideas of moral reason, duty, and justice itself are capable of exercising over the mind of a child, and he shows that it is wrong always to employ reward and punishment as educational devices, because that strengthens and confirms the student's egoistic impulses. There is certainly something true about this — and yet the fact that reward and punishment, praise and blame, exemplar and imitation, along with the ground of solidarity, sympathy, and love upon which their effect depends, that all these still form the "ethos" of humankind prior to all appeals to reason and thus make such appeals possible in the first place: this is the heart of Aristotle's ethics, and Kant does not do it justice. The limitations that necessarily underlie our insight into what is morally right do not have to lead to that corrupt mixture of motives that Kant exposed. In particular, ancient

eudaimonia—as distinct from the worldly wisdom of the Enlightenment—cannot be accused of heteronomy, of muddying
the transcendental purity of the moral. That is proved preeminently by the utopian rigorism of Plato's *Republic* (book 2).
Aristotle too does not for a moment overlook the fact that
people are concerned with justice for its own sake, and that
no considerations of a hedonistic, utilitarian, or eudaimonistic
kind can be allowed to prejudice the unconditionality of a genuine moral decision. Indeed, even the conditionedness of our insight—where what is concerned is not decision in the eminent
sense of the word, but rather the choice of the better (*prohairesis*)—represents in general no deficiency and no obstacle.
It has the social and political determinacy of the individual as
its positive content. This determinacy, however, is more than
dependence on the changing conditions of social and historical life. Everyone is undoubtedly dependent on the ideas of
their time and world, but from this follows neither the legitimacy of moral skepticism nor the exercise of political power in
the form of technical manipulation of opinion. The alterations
that transpire in morals and modes of thought that, especially
for the elderly, portend the utter dissolution of all morals, come
to pass upon an enduring basis. Family, society, and state determine the essential constitution of the human being, in that
its ethos replenishes itself with varying contents. Of course,
no one knows how to predict what might become of humankind and all its forms of communal life—yet this does not
mean that everything is possible, that everything is directed by
arbitrariness and caprice and can be determined by the powers
that be. There are things that are naturally right.[10] Against the
conditionedness of all moral knowledge by moral and political
being, Aristotle counterbalances the conviction that he shares
with Plato that the system of being is powerful enough to set

limits to all human confusion. Amidst all distortions, one idea remains indestructible: "How strong, though, is the polis by reason of its own nature."[11]

Thus Aristotle's ethics is able to take cognizance of the conditionedness of all human being without having to deny its own conditionedness. A philosophical ethics that is not only aware of its own questionableness in this way, but takes that very questionableness as one of its essential contents seems to me the only kind that is adequate to the unconditionality of the moral.

3

On the Divine in Early
Greek Thought (1970)

Our evidence concerning the earliest Greek meditations about the being of things as a whole makes it appear virtually certain that this being is also termed the divine (τὸ θεῖον).[1] The mythical world picture mirrored for us in Homer and Hesiod forms the background against which arise the Ionians' bold endeavors in thought. Epic ideas and concepts thus find their application and expression in the new knowledge. To that extent, Greek thought includes from its earliest beginnings an element of philosophical theology, especially as that is presented in Plato and Aristotle.

When we are speaking of the Greeks, philosophical theology means something completely different from what is later understood under the rubric of philosophical or natural theology, for this later concept is defined by its opposition to revealed theology and designates the truths about God that reason can discern by itself, without assistance from revelation. For Christian thought this raises a problem. It hardly accords with the dignity of religious revelation that humankind is of itself capable of discerning the truths of religion. Thus, given the claim of revelation, rational theology remains a source of conflict, especially among the various sects. Greek thought manifests no such problem. Greek religion is neither a religion of the book nor a religion of true doctrine, but rather a cultic tradition the theological systematization and integration of which are matters for poets—which is to say, for ongoing, nonbinding invention.

This is the way it looks to Herodotus and to those today for whom Homer and Hesiod represent the earliest literary tradition. If we have good reason to say that the first Ionian thinkers called ur-being "the divine," perhaps the indefiniteness of their manner of expression can serve to mirror the nonbinding quality which Greek boldness of thought claimed for itself vis-à-vis religious reality. On the other side, we can find assistance in the preference for the nominalized adjective with the definite article that early thought generally exhibits. Following Karl Reinhardt,[2] Bruno Snell[3] has extolled the special aptness of the Greek language when it employs the nominalized neuter in order to express a conceptual abstraction, which the Greeks do continually, as it were, on the way to the concept. What we call being, moreover, the Greeks term τὰ ὄντα or τὰ πάντα,[4] and they begin the march toward the concept when Parmenides reformulates the collective meanings implied in these expressions in the singular τὸ ὄν. If the "divine" is to be met with early on in the tradition, prior to the Ionians, this is the anticipation of the first concept of unity and being.

Thus talk of the divinity of being seems at first glance to mean nothing but this concept of the whole, here raised to the status of an object of philosophy's bold questioning and fundamentally distinguished from all the other appearances that we call existing (seiend), just as much as the gods' form of existence is distinct from that of mortals. Only the visible eternity of the heavens can share the predicate of divinity with the concept of the whole. Aristotle still appeals to the religious parallel when he presents the new astronomy of his time in the doctrine of the souls or spirits that move the heavens.[5] The pride of the new forms of thought is that they can integrate the religious tradition with their new knowledge. That, admittedly, cannot occur without "purifying" the religious tradition. Just as the whole of Greek poetry is a history of purifying the representations of the gods in the epics, so philosophy too undertakes the task of purification, in that it eliminates anthropomorphic elements from the representation of the gods and tries to ascertain only those things that are verifiable in thought. By the word "mythic" Aristotle refers to all those ways of representing the Olympian gods that view them as living beings in human forms, and he pointedly asks, for example, what good nectar and ambrosia are really supposed to do for the Olympians? Such things reduce the Olympians' self-sufficiency and independence and make them seem no more than magnified human beings, and this explains why all the speeches of the "theologians" have no interest for philosophical thought.[6]

Thus it seems that a homogenizing, enlightenment move is what holds the Greek thinkers together. The religious vocabulary that they took over, and especially the predicate of divinity, is not intended to make a statement about god or the gods, but rather to designate the order of being about which they are inquiring: the whole, the all, being.[7] Even when we do not forget that in precisely this period new religious movements were taking hold in Greece—these acquired their own religious existence alongside the official religion, in the form of the mystery cults and the so-called Orphic movement—nothing appears less likely than that Greek philosophy arises from the spirit of mysticism (as Karl Joël once maintained[8]). So too, the analogues drawn from the history of religion that Cornford[9] in particular used to interpret the most ancient Greek thinkers ultimately conceal the uniqueness of this origin. The grand mystery of initiation that frames Parmenides' educational poem, for example, has scarcely any religious quality. The illuminating doctrine which the goddess there proclaims—the being that is "thought," and so on—contrasts all too sharply with this religious-sounding illumination. Quite the contrary, we are reminded of the critique of the traditional representation of the gods to be found in almost every early thinker, in Xenophanes as in Parmenides and Heraclitus, not to speak of the wave of those like Anaxagoras influenced by Sophism.

Under these conditions, what does it mean that, in Plato as in Aristotle, being—that is, what in the fullest sense is (τὸ παντελῶς ὄν[10]) or what is in such a way that it is distinguished from all other beings by its continuous presence (in Aristotle's terms, what is ἐνέργεια without δύναμις)—is not only termed divine but life is expressly predicated of it? I have devoted another study[11] to the relationship between self-movement (life) and thought in early Greek thought, and this study found its strongest support in Anaxagoras's text on *nous*, which divides and distinguishes itself from itself. There I left open the question whether Plato and Aristotle ascribed a "living quality" to being for philosophical reasons or because of pre-ontological truisms and naive presuppositions. Here I would like to consider just this question.

There are primarily two specially marked passages that bear on this question, one in Plato, the other in Aristotle. The first is *Sophist* 248–9. Under discussion here are those who are called friends of the Ideas, who therefore absolutely divide the realm of true being from all becoming. It is being proved to them that knowledge of being signifies its becoming known and that movement is therefore involved in being. They, however, decline to admit that knowing and being known amount to action and passion—and here they are right insofar as what distinguishes the knowledge relation is that it does not alter the object that it grasps, but grasps it as it is "in itself." The twin categories of action and passion do not do justice to the reality of knowing. Knowledge must in every case find its own legitimacy for being. This is the question. And so the text proceeds: "But tell me, in heaven's name, are we really to be so easily convinced that change, life, soul, understanding have no place in that which is perfectly real—that it has neither life nor thought, but stands immutable in solemn aloofness, devoid of intelligence?" (Cornford trans.) With this question the refutation of the concept of being held by the friends of the Ideas has won the day. No one can take this seriously. Being must have nous; that is, there must be knowledge; so it seems obvious that it also has life and soul and thus movement as well.

This passage has been often discussed.[12] The Hegelian wing of neo-Kantianism viewed it as Plato's admission that the Ideas must be in movement. What is odd about this course of thought, however, is that it seems to be an argument *ad hominem*. Is it really so obvious that what truly is has movement, life, and spirit? Is Plato relying here only on common opinion, as he did, for example, when he conceptualized the "world" of the *Timaeus*—despite all the brilliant mathematics which the demiurge used in constructing it—as what was quite obviously an immense living being? Is this truism of an early mythical world view—notwithstanding the whole impulse toward enlightenment in Greek thought—simply a leftover that retained vestigial validity for Plato and his readers?

No less remarkable is the development that Aristotle's doctrine of the highest beings undergoes in *Metaphysics* Λ 7. There the necessity of a highest mover, who is himself unmoved, is derived from the system of being and movement of the All. What exists in this way causes motion like one's beloved and thus, without being itself moved, causes the movement of the whole: this statement is not intended to imply anything about the being of this highest being, but only to express the form of its movement.[13] In it the ceaseless cycle of the constellations has its origin. Its own constancy necessarily excludes all nonbeing and must therefore have a kind of eternal presence from which movement is likewise excluded, because in the case of something moved it would not be true in every sense that it is "already in existence" (*schon da*). Thus it must be a being that moves without being moved itself. This course of thinking is conclusive, and it seems less an argumentative confirmation of it than a superficial description when suddenly the mode of being of this highest mover is compared to our own: its activity is described like that of nous, which makes itself understood, and which therefore has life and the blessedness of pure intuition. This passage too gives the appearance of saying something obvious, requiring no proof that what exists forever in this way possesses the quality of being alive.

The similarity of the two passages sets us our task. How can being be understood such that its having life and spirit can be presumed obvious. To view this as the vestige of a naive world view that at the end of the great history of the Greek enlightenment suddenly breaks through again—Anaxagoras thought the sun was a glowing stone—would be to underestimate the energy of this new thought. At the very least, we would need to ask how such a naive supposition from a traditional world of ideas insinuated itself into the whole of what is conceived as the meaning of being in Platonic as well as Aristotelian thought.

At this point we need to go back to the beginning. What early Greek thought was attempting to investigate with incomparable boldness was the whole of being. We have reason to believe that one of the oldest riddles occupying these men was this: how does the whole of being "hold" itself (sich . . . "hält": also, "comport" or "behave") if there is no longer an Atlas to hold up the sky, and every new Atlas that could be substituted in his place—whether water with Thales, air with Anaximenes, or whatever—merely postpones the problem. Aristotle's victorious arguments had shown that the behavior (*Sich-Halten*) of water that is supposed to swim upon the earth presents no less of a problem than the behavior of the earth itself.[14] When we examine the documents that have come down to us, we get the impression that the early thinkers would have need of no such remonstrance. Our evidence all points in a different direction: namely, that they took as their conceptual frame a contrary kind of *Sich-Halten:* a form of balance among the various component parts constituting the whole. In Anaximander this seems to have taken on plainly geometrical forms.[15] Here for the first time arises the new idea in Greek thought, which Aristotle has analyzed as φύσις: the being that has its ἀρχὴ τῆς κινήσεως in itself. At any rate, we can say that the reigning idea from Thales to Plato's *Phaedo* is that the being of the whole "holds" itself.

This conceptual motif set a task whose solution kept early thinkers breathless. It seems certain that the earliest thinkers among the Greeks had no other name for the whole than the "All" (τὰ πάντα).[16] This is a collective concept still lacking in any unifying element. If it is "balance" that constitutes the structure of the "All" for these early thinkers, a balance that produces (and proves itself in bringing about) a reconciliation among various forces, then it truly does imply an intuitive form of unity. It becomes explicit for the first time in the process of interpretation and response with which Eleatic philosophy engaged that initiative. The denial of multiplicity as well as the denial of movement taught by the Eleatics gain depth for the first time in conceptualizing the unity of the All. Yet here too we find no real concept of unity that would allow the uniqueness of a being to be understood. Even such a contested and, in Greek doxography, pedantically articulated doctrine as that of the limitedness and limitlessness of the All—according to the documents that have come down to us, it was even presented in various ways within the Eleatic "school" (Parmenides, Melissos)—offers indirect proof that the unity of the whole was still entirely lacking in conceptual clarity.[17] Clearly, both statements—that of Melissos and that of Parmenides—make sense and indicate no genuine difference within learned opinion. It is telling that even Aristotle can accept linguistic usage to the effect that the whole is what οὗ μηδέν ἐστι ἔξω (*Physics* Γ 6, 207a8)—which is virtually to admit that everything is comprehended within it, so that in going through it one never arrives at a limit, and thus it is "endless." Moreover, it is only after Parmenides, in Zeno's indirect lines of argument and especially in the critique of the Eleatics in Plato's dialogues, that the concept of the ἕν begins to supplement that of the ὄν and finally supplants it completely. It could be shown that the philosophy of Plato was the first to succeed in conceptually grounding the unity of the All "posited" in Parmenides.

In Plato's *Timaeus* we read of this grounding. But how remarkable it is! The explicators of *Timaeus* 31a always have a hard time with the passage. It runs as follows: "Are we right in saying that there is one world, or that there are many and infinite? There must be one only if the created copy is to accord with the original. For that which includes all other intelligible creatures cannot have a second or companion, etc." (Jowett trans.). What an argument this is! What is made by following a model can therefore be only one? This, even if we ignore the self-contradiction that, by being imitated, the model necessarily ceases being the one and only being—as if the unity of the original were not precisely what makes possible the multiplicity of its imitations. In the same way, Aristotle, quite reasonably from this point of view, grounds the singleness of the All by comparing it to using up everything. It is convincing to say that if nothing more is left to create other worlds, there must remain the one and only world. But this is not primarily what is at issue;[18] it is rather the similarity between the world according to the will of god and a perfect living being. The reason Plato considers his argument conclusive can lie only in the fact that here two presuppositions are combined with each other: first, in producing something, the anticipation of what is to be produced receives its fulfillment. The meaning of all imitation is fulfilled in the "perfect" representation of the imitated. It is pointless to repeat it any more when the first attempt at imitation is perfectly successful. This is an argument that does nothing to further Plato's concept of μίμησις, for as Plato conceives it, the μίμησις remains in principle secondary to the model (and he therefore ascribes "the many" to imitations of the *eidos*). Now, the all-encompassing is what is supposedly being produced here. That the imitation of what is all-encompassing must itself be all-encompassing, and must therefore preclude a second imitation, remains a weak argument, logically viewed—as if imitations have not always "strived" to be what they admired. The argument becomes conclusive, however, if one views this imitation as the work of a divine *techne* that creates what is best and therefore leaves no room for a second try at imitating. Admittedly there is nothing directly about this in the text. But it is to be found in what immediately precedes it (30a6 ff.)[19]—and this passage implies no more or less than this: what is produced as the ἄριστον ἔργον of the "best" must be nous in soul and soul in body—that is, a reasoning living being—and in what follows it becomes manifest what all is implied in the demiurge's intent and πρόνοια. Again and again what emerges is the same thing: for example, in the creation of time, where the insuperable difference between model and copy bears the entire weight of the analysis, especially in the discussion of the subordinate gods, who create the lesser things that are always destined for dissolution. The world and the gods, by contrast, remain exempt from dissolution. The world's unity of being is conceived via its having the form of a reasonable living being; moreover, the fable of the divine techne serves to make this unity as such explicit—that is, as the one comprehensive whole, as the projection of an artist.[20]

Both sequences of thought, the self-supporting (*sich hal-*

tenden) whole and the unity of the whole that is projected in advance, come to be conceived adequately only when the unity is no longer based on a collection of scattered things, but is rather the unity of things belonging to and united with each other through and through: in the *Timaeus* it is the "world soul" which, as what comprehends all and holds it together, functions to unify the whole; and how thoroughly this is formed by the "logical" categories of identity and difference, we will now consider. Nevertheless, what is here under discussion is clearly the idea of a living thing and especially the "world animal," and in this context other ideas of animals are to be met with. I cannot understand how people can so mishandle the context of the *Timaeus* as to derive from it the "dynamic character of the cosmos of ideas."[21] To repeat, what "dynamic" means here we learn not from the fables of the *Timaeus,* but from the dialectic of kinds in the *Sophist.*

Now it certainly may have been just to help in explicating this concept of unity that the whole of beings whose being is in question here took the place formerly occupied by the Olympic deities. It is true, as we have emphasized above, that early Greek thought is consistently motivated by the endeavor to overcome the anthropomorphism threatened thereby and to exclude mythical ideas; but this also demonstrates precisely how seductive were such anthropomorphizing extrapolations. Thus, as a few parallel texts show, the verse of Xenophanes—"he sees all, he perceives all, he hears all" (B 24 in Diels)—is clearly intended to remove everything of human form from the image of being, and it is probably evident that his statements on the character of god are not an early Greek anticipation of monotheism; rather, they signify the whole of beings that the Ionians had made the object of their thought and inquiry. The verse means: So little does the divine being have human form that it lacks all special organs of sensation. How ambiguous this is! What kind of image is supposed to be evoked: a spherical world animal that takes in things with its entire skin? Or the omnipresence of being that exists nowhere more or less? At any rate, even in the attempt to avoid it, the language of anthropomorphic theology continues to be spoken.

The didactic poem by Parmenides, by contrast, seems completely free of this kind of thing. It is nevertheless the case here that being—of course in the full strictness of the course of thought—is found to be connected as closely as possible with "thought," specifically in the way that νοεῖν and εἶναι intrinsically belong together. However obscure in detail the meaning of Parmenides' thesis about identity remains, the exclusion of the nothing as something inconceivable still allows the meaning of this identity to become discernible in the sense that what is, never is not—that is, it is present for those who are acquainted with it. In understanding this, all appeals to an idealistic tradition are misplaced. It does not begin from "thought"; what it is about is being—that is, the way what exists is, and this includes its being such that one is acquainted with it as present. That is the meaning of νοεῖν: the immediate exposure to the There, which may also constitute the meaning of Nous in the verse of Xenophanes, where seeing and hearing are eulogized.

If we follow this thread still further, it becomes completely clear that when Plato renews the motif of the living quality of being, he is not so much conserving or reverting to an earlier tradition as furthering the effort of "Eleatic" thought. For what Plato demonstrates in direct counterpoint to the conclusions of the Greek enlightenment, especially in book X of the *Laws* entitled "Psyche," is not limited to the self-relatedness of living beings that is expressed in self-initiated motion (αὐτοκινοῦν seems to be one of Plato's neologisms). The analysis of ten kinds of movement in the *Laws* (X, 893b–894d) indeed singles out such self-movement. It is the tenth and last of the kinds differentiated there, and clearly this is where the whole course of thought is headed. At last, it is in truth the first — that is, the real origin of all movement. This becomes explicit in contrast to Anaxagoras, clearly because the latter had not discussed the soul when he ascribed being-in-motion to nous. Admittedly Plato, by contrast, also emphasizes elsewhere — in emphatic detail, for example, in *Timaeus* 37c2 — that the place of nous is only in the psyche. This does not alter the fact, however, that Plato typically furthers the direction of Eleatic thought and discerns the structure of being in the logical structuration of thought (the logos).

Thus it becomes clear what both passages with which we began really mean: Plato calls what exists fully τὸ παντελῶς ὄν (*Sophist* 248c). This combination of words may well furnish something like an ontological pointer, for the usual word παντελῶς is here combined with what seems to a naive consciousness not susceptible of degree: being. Plato recognizes an ontological comparative. At any rate, the context prohibits us from understanding τὸ παντελῶς ὄν as synonymous with τὰ πάντα, so that movement occurs in being also. No, life and movement must be in precisely that which, in a preeminent sense, is. Confirming this is the linguistic usage of the *Timaeus* where it speaks of παντελῶς ζῷον (30b1) and describes this ζῷον as κατὰ πάντα τελέῳ (30d2) — the content of which is again explained in 30b5 as ὅπως ὅτι κάλλιστον εἴη. . . . Thus it is described as a "being" (*Seiendes*) but in a way that distinguishes its "being" (*Sein*) from that of other beings (*Seienden*). What comprehends all is not just "everything," but rather the One that comprehends "everything." In the *Timaeus* this is introduced via the idea of natural living being, and it is shown that movement and life and soul belong to the predicates of the All. Here, however, as in the *Sophist*, everything points to the nous, for the being-known of being is what ultimately proves that there must be movement in the Ideas. The movement here ascribed to being must, therefore, be derived from the movement of the logos, and not from the presupposition of its vitality or divinity. That is what poses the real question: what is this movement that is called thinking?

According to the doctrine of movement in the *Laws*, book X, it is no matter of immediate observation, but rather (as in the famous passage of the *Phaedo*, 99d) it is compared to looking at the sun and only the reflection of it being captured in the eye. When Socrates uses the same image in the *Phaedo* in order to justify his flight into the logoi—that is, his dialectical procedure—the irony with which he there treats embarking on this second-best journey is clear enough. The logoi are not a mere copy of visible reality; just the opposite, this reality is in fact a mere copy of that whose true object is thought. Here, however, the outwardly visible circling movement is really nothing but a mere copy of the movement of nous. This proves that Plato is continuing Socrates' journey through the logoi. This explains the existence of a statement about the movement of nous without the irony regarding this image that Plato often employs elsewhere about the way such spatial images represent matters. The circling, spinning movement of a top that remains in one place and rotates around a fixed middle is what Plato considers most similar of all to the "movement" of nous.

The logical task presented by the image of the top is apparent. It serves to formulate perceptually what in logic we call a "contradictory proposition," and by means of a perceptible model it succeeds in exposing as merely apparent the contradictions created by the new sophistic art of thought. In this way Plato represents the structure of the logos, which can cause confusion and enable us to recognize what is. It is hardly surprising that it requires an image, for the concepts that he has at his disposal are not at all appropriate to this theme of reflection; rather, they are suited to express things we encounter in the "world." Plato's task, however, is to use the old means to defend the new path of dialectic—that is, the journey via the logoi. Thus the new emerges next to the old. In the *Sophist* the new relationship between the determinations of pure reflection, identity, and difference aligns itself with the old opposition between rest and movement.

When the different is predicated of the same, only empty sophism takes this for a contradiction, and in such propositions the essence of the dialectician consists in distinguishing the various aspects of the proposition. The dialectician knows how to hold onto the identical and to think the changing in its changefulness. What is involved here is the structure of a relation. The being of the relative (πρός τι) exists in such a way that it consists in being taken in a certain respect. Only when this comes to be understood can we dispel the uneasiness that the phenomenon of the relative occasions in thought. For Sophism appears persuasive because it discerns contradictions at precisely the point where one has this insight into the structure of deductive discourse: self-sameness and difference are essentially interwoven, and the relativity of propositions is to be explained by appeal to the different respects in which they are taken. Thinking means holding onto the same as the same in its changing aspects. This implies that the same as same has the character of a relation. The interwovenness of sameness and difference depends on the fact that of itself the same cannot be thought without difference. In fact, this logical illumination of the enigmatic and confusing phenomenon of the new art of thought disseminated by Sophism brought the line of Greek thought about being which we have been following came to its culmination and end.

For it is obviously more than an image to say that the movement of thought corresponds to the circling movement of a top or a ball rotating on a lathe. In book X of the *Laws*, it is introduced as a kind of image, to be sure, but the same analogy is proposed in the *Timaeus* (34a) without any emphasis being placed on its being an image. Of course, what is generally being discussed there is a myth. Nevertheless, it is from the movement of thought that the ball shape of the rotating world totality is derived. Thus the remarkable course of thought in book X of the *Laws* must be evaluated according to the probative claim it makes. It is there that self-movement is deemed to be first and most primordial among the ten types of movement, and ascribed to the psyche, to the living being. Finally, however, this self-movement, defined as belonging to the whole system of heavenly movements, is given the name of nous in its "standing" movement. Thus, it is from the presupposition of a soul with reason that orders all things well that the divinity of the constellations is first inferred. Thus, ultimately it is everywhere the case in Plato that the self-moving soul finds its true being in νοεῖν, in the apprehension of the Ideas (*Phaedrus*); and this involves holding onto the same just as much as the different. One need only remember how in the *Philebus* the nous fulfills the regal function of uniting all but also seems in a position to divide and differentiate all. Self-movement is ultimately self-differentiation.

Most important here is that the noetic nature of the world is the only thing that makes it accessible to thought. When Plato ascribes "soul" to the world, he is referring to the self-movement of a whole which, as stated expressly in *Laws* 898c, is not perceivable but can only be thought. In fact, even an observable movement is never seen as such; rather, only in thought can it be realized that something moves itself of itself. Yet among movements of this kind there is a special one distinct from all other finite movements through the regularity of its coming and going, the circling movement of the heavenly bodies.

In order to distinguish this circular movement that is undifferentiated at the beginning and end, it makes sense to confer on the soul (which is what is in motion here) a distinctive quality, and that is nous. The way living beings that are characterized by appeal to the concept of soul come to fulfillment, according to Plato, consists in their being concerned for what has no soul (*Phaedrus* 246b6: ψυχὴ πᾶσα παντὸς ἐπιμελεῖται τοῦ ἀψύχου). The soul that concerns itself with the course of the All does so, as its orderliness (*Geordnetheit*) shows, with noetic perfection—that is, it proceeds under the guidance of nous.

At the same time, there is really no right answer to the question of why the demiurge, itself perfect, does not organize everything in concentric orbits. But that certainly means overestimating the explanatory claim of Plato's "physics." The ecliptic and the anomalous movements of the planets are the given that the tale of the demiurge elaborates. The tale is merely intended to explain the possibility of these phenomena, and this happens by their being remarkably grounded on a dialectic among the highest determinations of reflection. Just as everything fluctuates with the movement of the world according to the rhythm of the seasons, yet ever again recreates the system of the whole, difference and sameness are both there in being, existently there (the *Timaeus* 35a describes this *Da-Sein* as a "mixture" of being, sameness, and difference). This "explains" not only the construction of the visible world; the infinite multiplicity of altering appearances is fundamentally opened to thought. Those who try to think being as that which is—that is, in its sameness—must think it in its difference from itself, in its variations. But to possess self-difference means to stand in different relationships. In the unfolding of such relations, the whole of being continually presents itself otherwise, yet remains one and the same. It is self-identical being at the same time as it is the totality of its differences. Just as the rotating top presents itself as one fixed thing and in truth allows the multiplicity of its differences—that is, its aspects—to flow together in the unity of its appearance, so it is for everything that exists aspectually: the totality of all aspects in which it is are copresent. What comes to stand there in the most various relations is, as the phrase has it, "one and the same." So it is a genuine unity of being and being thought that Plato describes in explicating Parmenides' profundity. It is this, and not imaginary folklore, that grounds his saying that all true beings are alive.

Moreover, a higher concept of unity gleams through the conceptual scheme of Plato's dialectic: the relationship of the one and the many, as the *Philebus* shows, is not the trivial relationship of the one and its parts. The meaning of unity comes to consummation only when its inner relation to multiplicity is thought at the same time. From this the concept of unity derives its proximity to the concept of the whole. Here too the whole and the part exist in dialectical unity. Wholeness can exist only where there are parts, but parts are not separate pieces of something conglomerated together in a pile. Instead, a part is what belongs to a thing in such a way that without it something would be missing and it would be maimed.[22] The glance at living beings here guides the process of logical concept formation, but the logical relation among concepts is what is in view. The phenomenon of life can be heard in Plato's phrase μέρη καὶ μέλη, but clearly it is the defining elements of the logos at which this phrase is aiming. The construction of the soul, as of the world, consists in sameness and difference being woven together.

An inquiry similar to the one we have here undertaken of the passage in the *Sophist* needs now to be initiated with respect to the second passage that we have taken as fundamental, the one in Aristotle's *Metaphysics*. The course of thought there is almost more surprising, because with cosmological sagacity Aristotle derives the highest mover from the systematic movement of the whole, and then suddenly characterizes it not only as living but as taking pleasure in looking. Certainly the highest mover is raised above all comparison when Aristotle grounds the continuity of beings in the whole system of its being and movement. What moves thus and continues in movement must itself be unmoved and cannot move in the same way as everything else that moves things—that is, such that it is moved itself—because it cannot, like that which is moved, be always becoming something different. Thus it is only a short step to predicating divinity of this special being. Actually, in the older tradition of Greek thought displaced by the Homeric world picture, this is an entirely conventional motif. In Aristotle, however, distinguishing the prime mover via the idea of god is more than just passing down a tradition. Rather, he consciously takes a position in relation to that tradition, because of his claim to have grounded it in a new way.

In this way Aristotle is very probably taking cognizance of a counterposition; he is opposing the view, represented by the Pythagoreans and Plato's student Speusippus, that the beautiful and the perfect are not the beginning and origin of being; rather, the orderliness of the whole that rests upon eternal mathematics is the completed result and end. This means neither more nor less than this: the perfect is not something eternal existing for itself. Plato's *Timaeus*, too, is only telling a tale of the creation of the world, and the real meaning of the world soul forged there is that for the most part the universe obeys mathematical laws.

Now, being alive is not the only characteristic that distinguishes the prime mover. All the spirits of the spheres in Aristotelian cosmology are bound to the heavenly bodies and guide them like souls. It is difficult, however, to interpret the statements about the highest mover as general characteristics of such spirits. The relation between the highest mover and these other spirits remains unusually obscure in Aristotle. There is still another difficulty here, however. Theophrastus had already insisted in the aporias of his *Metaphysics* that the prime mover cannot be defined by reference to self-movement alone if it also acts as motive, as the object of love and striving. For this is presumably to ascribe the ability to strive to everything that strives for the highest—but this implies that the nature of its being is life and self-relatedness.[23] This is convincing. On the other hand, it is not at all obvious that the object of this striving must likewise be alive and self-related. Clearly the Pythagoreans and Speusippus thought quite otherwise when they singled out mathematical harmony as the object imitated by all.

There is a third difficulty explicated by Aristotle that cannot be explained away as a conventional adaptation from theology. Aristotle says that there can be nothing to which this highest being is alien, nothing that can be independent of it, because otherwise the highest being would depend on this object. If it follows therefrom that the highest being can be within no other but only itself, this consequence is truly intelligible only if we keep in mind the argument originating with the Eleatics about the identity of being and being-within (εἶναι and νοεῖν). That is, no more than Plato does Aristotle repeat the older theological cosmology. What he is aiming at is not endowing the essence of all being with the predicates of divinity, but rather envisioning what being in general really is in terms of what persists, unaltered in itself and unmoved.

This is also confirmed in the analysis of what Aristotle calls being true (ὂν ὡς ἀληθές). It becomes completely clear in the discussion of *Metaphysics* Θ 10 how being and being-within belong together.

This passage shows that the "what," or essence, since it is simple and does not consist of an assemblage, cannot be anything but true, if only it in general is intended. It is in this way that it differentiates itself from propositional truths that always join one thing with another and so are capable of joining things which by the nature of the case do not belong together. To describe how essence is true (*das Wahrsein des Wesens*) Aristotle employs the image of touching (θιγγάνειν). This is what permits me to use the German word *Innesein* (knowing, or being within) for νοεῖν. For when Aristotle says that an intention of the "what" is always "true," and that thinking and what is thought (νοεῖν and νοητόν) are the same whenever such a "what" is thought, an expression such as *Innesein* suggests itself to us. Usually we call such a thing a feeling. By this we mean, too, that what is felt cannot be at all distinguished from the feeling of it. It obviously makes no sense to distinguish between the intended content of the feeling and the condition of having the feeling. The semantic field of the Greek word θιγγάνειν points in the same direction. The word is used preeminently for "touching with the hand" and comprehends the immediacy with which one becomes aware (*inne wird*) that something exists.

The German word *Innesein* admittedly has very different connotations from those heard in the Greek νοεῖν. Such words are formed by subjectivist thinking and the history of inwardness. To that extent the German word can stand in for the Greek conceptual term only in a provisional way. But proposing *Innesein* as a translation enables us to show that what is meant here is an experience of being, not an act of the subject. In this way we can see how the primordial intuition of the Eleatics—that "thinking" and "being" belong together—is of fundamental significance for Attic philosophy. The experience of being, then, is what brings in all the predicates of life and divinity that we encounter with a certain logical surprise in Aristotle's text. It is not the case that the naive persistence of religious traditions brings something undemonstrable by thought into thought about being. The logical quintessence of this train of thought lies in this: being thought (*Innegehabtsein*) of itself advenes to being, because self-relatedness is the fundamental nature of being. Only in this way can it be shown why predicates such as life and self-movement, themselves having the structure of self-relatedness in turn, can be ascribed to being.

To return to the inner connection between self-movement and self-relatedness or -differentiation: by beginning with the *Charmides* in my essay "Vorgestalten der Reflexion" (see note 11) I have been able to establish a few things that shed new light particularly on the speculation about nous beginning with Anaxagoras. The present inquiry has, I believe, gone further in showing that the connection between being and life always plays a part in the philosophical thought of the Greeks.

What looked like a mere *theologumenon* proves to be a consequence of philosophical considerations. The problematic of the prime mover is connected to the fact that it is distinguished by having the quality of life and enjoying the blessedness of beholding—and this connection does not depend on the truth of the new philosophy that Hegel formulated. Rather, it depends on the structure of the logos in which being presents itself in its unity and multiplicity.

4

The Ontological Problem
of Value (1971)

The German philosophical tradition considers itself the first to have paid attention to the so-called value philosophy whose influence reaches all the way from the world of Latinity to today, and this in such a way that we are submitting its conceptual basis, the concept of value, to historical inquiry. The purpose is not to increase our historical knowledge, but to make us aware of the intrinsic implications involved in using the concept of value. What is at issue is not only the well-known distinction between fact and value that is especially dominant in southwest neo-Kantianism and the way it influences the social sciences (Max Weber). The present-day discussion shows that this distinction is pointless on the level of reflection we have reached today—especially after the dogmatism of the concept of "fact" has been critiqued by theory of science, hermeneutics, and ideology critique. On the other side, the German phenomenology of value from Brentano to Husserl, Scheler, and Nicolai Hartmann presents the opportunity to reinterpret the Catholic doctrine of goods and virtues, and thus also of "philosophia perennis." Now, as before, this has real currency, which makes the ontological question about "value" worth discussing.

Here, I think, we glimpse the methodological limits of language analysis as a mode of discussion. What is at issue is not just the question of how normative propositions and value judgments can have a logical legitimacy on a par with that of theoretical propositions, but whether a normative claim like that ascribed to "value" is legitimate—that is, whether it possesses a binding, obligatory "being" independent of the valuer. The ontological aspect of the value problem presents a narrows that cannot be made passable by avoiding the whole line of questioning about the ontological claim of "value." In truth, the concept of value is the expression of a genuine philosophical embarrassment that impels us to undertake philosophical self-reflection. Ultimately everyone must admit that the background of this philosophical embarrassment is constituted by a common element of our culture: namely, the role that modern empirical science plays in the life and consciousness of present-day humankind. From the viewpoint of empirical methodology —its principle of hypothesis and verification, which makes the object world subject to being altered and reproduced by human planning and work—the normative viewpoint seems inaccessible and closed. The primary values and purposes that are supposed to direct and control our knowledge and abilities are not themselves susceptible to being communicated or justified by modern science, the common basis of all contemporary philosophy.

The fundamental tension of our philosophical consciousness manifests itself likewise in the history of the value problem as it occupied the thought of the nineteenth and twentieth centuries. The problem of value, as it emerged in the victorious progress of philosophy of science in the nineteenth century and then came to define the neo-Kantianism of Windelband and Rickert, needs to be worked out once more by returning to Kant himself. Kant's distinction between the sensible and the intelligible world, and especially his treatment of the problem of freedom on the basis of this distinction, precisely indicates the new task facing thought once it relinquished the Christianity-based teleology of the created world. The consequence of the *Critique of Pure Reason* was to show persuasively that a priori conditions underlie human experience which clarify what matter governed by laws is and thus what constitutes the concept of nature. How the nature of freedom is to be explained given the dominion of natural laws—to this question theoretical reason can offer no answer. Yet freedom is a fact of reason (*Vernunftfaktum*)—as Kant calls it in a consciously paradoxical formulation—for he ascribes the empirical concept of fact to a "faculty of ideas," that is, to reason. According to the *Critique*—which had undermined the theoretical use of reason outside "possible experience," especially the teleological idea of a world conceptualized in terms of purpose and affirming humankind—the self-certainty of practical reason offers a new kind of firm foundation. The fact that duty obligates, and that such obligation can be understood only given the presupposition of freedom, carries an inherent certainty that necessitates consideration of reason's need for the unity of a whole, since it can never complete the endless progress of experience. Kant names this whole "the realm of purpose" and says it is a concept that is fruitful everywhere—obviously without wanting in the slightest to revive dogmatic teleology. On the contrary, this concept follows directly from freedom as a fact of reason, because there—and only there—the relativity of experience is transcended. The experience transcended, however, is not, ultimately, the experience that people have as people. The realm of purpose refers to the constitution of a world of reason that lies beyond all empirical values and judgments. The moral person—or, as Kant has it, good will—is distinct from everything else that is valued, so that it has an absolute value and is beyond price. Kant juxtaposes the concept of absolute or intrinsic value—which constitutes the worth of humanity and gives it the character of an end in itself—with the value concept that originates in English economics of the eighteenth century. All moral philosophy that begins with the concept of use, precisely insofar as it implies a social utilitarianism, and even the social reality of a "moral sense," was to be superseded when Kant grounded moral law in the concept of freedom. The paradoxical expression of this supersession is the concept of an "end in itself," as implied in well-known formulations of the categorical imperative: namely, that we are never permitted to treat other people as means, but instead must respect them as ends in themselves.

Insofar as a concept is connected with the term "value" here, it is defined entirely by its opposition to the relativity of value judgments postulated by utilitarian/eudaimonic moral philosophy, as Kant was acquainted with it, probably from Hume's careful summary of English moral sense philosophy. On the other hand, Kant's founding of morality does not revitalize the traditional doctrine of goods grounded in the order of creation; instead, it is built on a new, completely different foundation, from which it receives a "practical"—rather than a theoretical—legitimization. It would lead us too far afield were we to trace how Kant's other ideas on moral philosophy emerge from the unique evidence presented by the conditioned nature of moral law: that there is a realm of ends—because ends in themselves exist interdependently, so that the arbitrariness of each one is limited by acknowledging the others—and that there must be a highest end in this realm. This is the moral proof of God's existence, which Kant constructs with help from the doctrine of the highest good. In any case, the *Foundation of the Metaphysics of Morals* represents a reversal of the traditional sequence of legitimization. The moral law is not traced back to God; rather, God's existence follows from the moral law (in Kant's so-called postulatory metaphysics). This reversal of sequence signifies at once the autonomy of morality, its independence from worldly cleverness and fear of God, and it implies a strict differentiation between the natural world and the intelligible moral world, the one ruled by necessity, the other by freedom. Kant makes the claim that the way he grounds the independence of the moral consciousness stands in contrast to the whole tradition and presents the nature of morality in complete purity for the first time—that is, as a matter of practical reason. Thus he saw no real problem in the multiplicity, and possible collision, of duties taught by tradition: What duty is is the result of the moral self-examination of practical reason and as such is always only single. It gauges itself by the "form" of the will—that is, by the specific universality of the moral law.

Thus "law-examining reason"—to use Hegel's language—and in general the opposition between Ought and Is comes to take center stage in practical philosophy; and moral reality, the actual behavior of people in society and state, becomes a secondary problem. The fact that moral self-certainty is superseded by the doctrine of the postulates of practical reason and their development into a "moral world view," however, cannot really ground the broadening of moral reality in the life of human society. It has an inherently inescapable ambiguity. Is what the agent consoles himself with for the world's imperfection a mere idea (*Vorstellung*)—or is it even make-believe (*Verstellung*), behind which lies no real faith in a "moral world"? Hegel discovered this ambiguity early on and in particular recognized the limitations of Kant's legalistic view of the nature of love and the obligations of "objective spirit." In his *Phenomenology of Mind* he interprets the moral world view as well as the self-certainty of conscience as mere stages on the way to the self-recognition of mind that is realized in religion and philosophy.[1] So in Hegel's thought Kant's merely postulatory metaphysics was transformed into a real metaphysics of absolute spirit. This could now ground the moral world as a perfecting of reality—though, of course, it allowed Kant's "holy will" and "highest in the realm of ends" to dissolve into the all-encompassing unity of spirit.

Even within the school of Hegel itself, a theistic reaction against the pantheism of spirit worked itself out under Schelling's influence. It viewed itself as harking back to Kant. But there could be no mere return to Kant's duty-based morality after Hegel had shown its limits and raised them to philosophical consciousness. This is just as clear in Christian Wiesse as in Hermann Lotze. In both—as already earlier in Herbart—aesthetics acquires a new, systematic significance. Herein lies the background explaining why the concept of value played a new role in the nineteenth century. In certain ways this concept repeats the aporias that were connected with the concept of duty in traditional moral philosophy and that Kant had dissolved through the concept of the autonomy of practical reason. The problem of duty in relation to the many duties replicated itself in the relation between the unity of the thought about value and the multiplicity of values and presented itself as a tension between norms effective in society and a genuine moral decision undertaken in the conscience of the individual. But this tension no longer dissolves into practical reason and its categorical universalization of the moral law (as in Kant); instead, it is entrusted to the "variable judgment of feeling" (Lotze). Thus Hermann Lotze represents an "expanded view of the moral" that is grounded in the concept of beauty.[2]

In a work originating in 1845, "On the Concept of Beauty," Lotze details the factors giving rise to this expansion. He begins with Kant's *Critique of Judgment* and with the "pleasure" that stems not just from the play of cognitive faculties occasioned by our disinterested feeling of pleasure in the beautiful, but equally from the satisfaction of reason's need for unity that occurs with the help of so-called teleological judgment. It enables us to think of the system of nature as the unity of a whole. For Lotze, along with the beauty of individual things— in nature and art—emerges the beauty of the whole; both exist for reason, which Kant's critique of teleological judgment had already allied to aesthetic judgment under the common element of reflection. Lotze understands both as the reflective pleasure that is found in "beauty." This broad concept of beauty permits Lotze to juxtapose the beautiful with the good. Alongside the concept of what is unconditionally good that underlies all moral obligation emerges the worth of beauty as likewise evidently unconditioned. It too transcends the merely pleasant. Thus the concept of the unconditional good expands through the concept of the "understanding of what is in and of itself valuable," which in the experience of the beautiful points back to the "strictly moral."

Clearly, this is at the outset a theory that juxtaposes beauty and the obligating power of the moral. Even in Lotze's eyes the blessedness of the beautiful is related more to the holy than to the good. Beauty represents the reconciliation of is and ought, relief from the pain of should and of ends. This gives it a special systematic position. Even if it is apparent that echoes of moral values make art meaningful for us, unconditional value is a characteristic of the beautiful as well. Yet such an extension of moral unconditionality to the realm of art and beauty remains of only limited significance. Correct judgment of what is beautiful, and the flexibility of mind and imagination necessary to achieve it, cannot—as Lotze rightly emphasizes—be ascribed to everyone in the same way as correct judgment of what is one's duty. Lotze sees more deeply, moreover. He recognizes that what presses beyond the unconditionality of a moral consideration is itself originally morally motivated. "It is not just action that fulfills the definition of what is human"—a "spotlight of moral valuation" falls on our whole knowledge of the world.

Thus we think that it would not suffice for a higher significance of spiritual life merely to fulfill the general abstract demands of morality nor even to unite their individual elements in general harmony; on the contrary, for a higher moral seriousness it is necessary at the same time to pay attention to what is living and weaving itself out in the experiences of the existents and what is ripening toward future goals.

This is unmistakably similar to Kant's postulatory metaphysics. For Lotze too it is morality that, as "moral valuation," undergirds the whole and permits the harmony of the sensory and the moral world, of virtue and happiness, and permits even— in Lotze's phrase—the "sense of the world-all." Here we stand at the origin of the philosophical concept of value. The semantic facts say a great deal: as long as value emerges in connection with worth, worthiness, validity, sense, significance, even holiness, the idea has not basically developed beyond Kant's concept of the "absolute value" possessed by good will alone. Now, however, the plural—"values"—and the concept of a "realm of values" emerge, and therefore the problem of the "being" of these values emerges as well. What thus presents itself as a realm of values is of course no longer the realm of "ends in themselves" which constituted the intelligible world according to Kant's postulatory metaphysics; but it is nonetheless comparable to that realm of ends, in that "ends in themselves" circumscribe the arbitrariness of the individual. The same is true of values. What is "in and of itself valuable," and corresponds to the feeling that gives value or the reason that defines value, underlies a "distribution of values" that is not due to our arbitrariness but of itself demands acknowledgment. This is what grounds the task of "value philosophy" insofar as it develops a unique problematic.

The problem is clearly twofold. On the one hand, values

do not exist like facts but arise from the human institution of value; on the other, they stand in opposition to an individual's arbitrariness as the givens of our feeling that we are compelled to acknowledge. Clearly, this becomes intelligible by appeal to the beautiful: there would be no such thing apart from our "feeling spirit"—yet beauty moves us to wonder by way of its own superior being. Lotze affords us particular help in bringing together both sides of the experience of value, in that he broadens the moral through the beautiful. One must ascribe a certain arbitrariness and relativity to taste and preference, but on the other side, the highest beauty comes with an unconditionality that makes it rank alongside moral unconditionality.

This points to the problem with which an ethics of value had subsequently to concern itself: how to reconcile the relativity of values with their claim to be absolute and unconditional. In extending value philosophy to a material ethics of value, this problem took the following form: how does insight into value relations subsisting in themselves, insight into a hierarchy of values that can arise with the certainty of phenomenological evidence, square with the power of a living ethos that is itself hardly blind but, on the contrary, illuminated by practical reason? The question can also be formulated thus: must not insight into the realm of values and its ordering itself raise a claim to be the sole legitimate concrete ethos? This in fact shows up in the history of ethics of value. Already in 1864, following Lotze, the young Dilthey said that "increasing insight into value" would come to orient the morality of the future; and even more decisively in our century, Nicolai Hartmann, influenced by Scheler's material ethics of value, viewed philosophical knowledge of value as serving a maieutic function for our concrete consciousness of value. In both cases it is the same concrete ethos that is connected with research in value, and indeed that of a broader, more sensitive consciousness of value.

"On Passing By" was a chapter of Nietzsche that Hartmann followed like a motto. Indeed, only such an ethos is commensurate with the progress that is born of all research. Yet how can the idea of scientific progress be credibly extrapolated to the realm of value? In the age of liberalism this may well have been a conceivable illusion—Dilthey fell into it—but in our century it is obviously archaic.

The theory of values whose beginnings we have discerned in Lotze conceptualized the matter quite differently. Then, the connection between ethos and the realm of values was still completely obvious, so values have their origin in an ethos. For, according to Lotze, it is the ethos of living love that orders and unifies the realm of values. "Neither a realm of truths nor a realm of values is prior to living love."[3] Values subsisting in themselves exist only for those who feel, but it is precisely here that Lotze discerns living love: that a person sacrifices a value for a higher value, especially in willing the happiness of another. Appropriately, Lotze here too follows (even in his theology) Kant's postulatory doctrine, though of course he alters it in a characteristic manner: "Our concept of God too is insufficiently developed for beholding beauty to the extent that from his holiness it lets a moral world emanate, to be sure, but not a natural one."

Basically, this does not deviate from Kant in the slightest. On the universal basis of the moral proof of God, Kant too explained that the cosmological proof rooted in the purposefulness of the natural order was permissible only as an addition. For Lotze, admittedly, the task is much more difficult, because the theological basis of the order of creation had lost its persuasiveness in an age characterized by the victory of the natural sciences and the model of mechanics employed by all research into nature. So for Lotze the point, in his words, was to defend the "world of ends and forms" against the world of means.

That is the function for which Lotze developed the world of values—that is, the moral universe expanded to include beauty. Its purpose was to explain the world of forms.[4]

In the sequel, Lotze's naive synthesis of concrete ethos, as it obtains in human life, and the realm of values that rules the moral universe broke asunder. There is, first, the human power to institute values; on the other side, the pure insight into the system of what is "of value in and for itself." In the first direction lies the fundamental relativism of the values in which a given concrete ethos unfolds. Such a system can be considered from various viewpoints, depending on what is at a given time the "leading world view" according to which a given ethos articulates itself. Among the most significant examples of such inquiry, Marx's theory of ideologies, as well as Nietzsche's phrase about the revaluation of all values, are of decisive consequence. In the one case the material ethos is derived from social interests within a given situation—which implies that when this situation changes, the value system alters as well. In the other case the idea of the revaluation of all values is polemically directed against the world of Christian values which—even in the form secularized by the Idealism of "Hegel and the other Schleiermachers"—had lost its persuasive power in Nietzsche's eyes. The theoretical consequences of both critical positions are ultimately the same: relativistic. The system of values that articulates itself in various forms of ethos offers—for example, in Windelband, who was Hermann Lotze's student—merely a framework of materials for the cultural sciences, and however important to the social sciences was the spread of southwest German value philosophy, it never took up the philosophical task of mediating ethos and philosophical ethics. It intended to represent what was scientifically tenable in the heritage of Nietzsche's radicalism, and it is indicative that, in presenting the problem of value in his well-known textbook on the history of philosophy, Windelband begins with Nietzsche's moral philosophy. So we read in Nietzsche himself[5] a very instructive remark in which he not only recommends study of moral history and physiological exposition of existing tables of value, but also fundamentally raises the question "What is value for?" — that is, he demands that we work out the appropriate viewpoint for value in a given instance. In Nietzsche, of course, this is not really meant to be as relativistic as it sounds. When he writes that the task of philosophers is "to solve the problem of value and define the rank order of values," he is not at all proposing research that would make the domain of values into an object of knowledge. In any case, his intention is not relativistic; he demands, on the contrary, that the one unique ascendant viewpoint be worked out, which he himself defends against a morality based on *ressentiment:* "Beyond good and evil . . . this does not in the least mean 'beyond good and bad.'" Thus, value relativism is a theoretical consequence of Nietzsche's thought, but he himself intends to make the true order of values manifest by "beginning with life."

And now the other side: the special nature of the knowledge of value that Lotze emphasized, the recognition of something as being of value in itself, even though in the manner of feeling. This is where the phenomenological school ties in. Franz Brentano in fact grounds the unity of a class of psychic phenomena comprehending willing and feeling in their relation to the value or valuelessness of objects; and by expounding this in emphatic analogy to the recognition of true and false in a considered judgment, he derives from "love" and "hate" the "distribution of value" that Lotze explicitly recognized as being founded otherwise than on our preferences. The extent to which Brentano has Lotze in mind is shown by the especially numerous references to him in *Psychology from an Empirical Standpoint* (1874). Thus Brentano created the axioms of a phenomenological ethics of value by analyzing the phenomena of love and hate as relations to value and deriving the primary laws that obtain between the two.

Recently, Alois Roth's presentation of Husserl's early lectures has shed new light on the history of this value-based ethics.[6] The way Husserl continually took positions on Brentano's axiological analyses shows how fully the task of a phenomenological ethics occupied him during the Göttingen period. In Max Scheler's great work of 1913-16, which of course had been foreshadowed in many of his essays, this ethics came to a public breakthrough. Neither author is content with analyzing the a priori construction of the realm of values according to their fundamental laws, but is instead engaged in drawing metaphysical consequences for their ethical absolutism and the objectivism of value. They climax in a philosophical teleology and theology, as Lotze too had in mind before. This solidifies the superiority of a value-based ethics to a goods-based ethics, and especially Kant's "reversal" of the relationship between moral philosophy and theology, or morality and religion. Husserl seems to go as far as possible in his a priori deduction of a *summum bonum formaliter spectatum* and in accepting an essential correlation between the highest person and the system of values in the world. God is conceived "as the idea of the most perfect life of all, in which is constituted the most perfect 'world' of all, from which is creatively developed the most perfect of all spiritual worlds in respect to a most perfect nature of all."[7] Ethics, then, refers to a "super-reality" that lets all empirical reality emerge supra-empirically. At the beginning, Scheler confidently accepted the idea of a highest person as the ultimate ground of the world—in order later to arrive at a theory of "spirit," thanks to studies in anthropology and philosophy of nature, without giving up the central place of the person in ethics—not only in the sense that the "personal act" is the center to which all validity of values returns, but also in the sense that the value adhering to persons is of an order obviously superior to all other dimensions of value. Even the moral development of the individual person succeeds practically in giving immediate access not to the "realm of values" but rather beyond the value of the person, as Scheler clearly recognized. Forming one's own ethos and the concrete ethical gestalt of a group occur beyond following models and ethical imitation, and only on the basis of such presuppositions can the domain of value become visible to itself.

Yet here the relation of ethos and knowledge in the "realm of values" remains unclear. The most logical, though also most one-sided, position to take on this question is clearly that advanced by Nicolai Hartmann. Hartmann not only views the task of value-based ethics as continually broadening the consciousness of value and thus gives it a relation to the concrete ethos; he also reflects on the relation to ethos again from the viewpoint of the idea of value.[8] That is, if we begin with the idea that values are "beheld" or "perceived" in objective universality and then actualized at a given time in concrete human behavior or in the value feelings embedded in praxis, our problem can be reduced to the general problem of judgment, which subsumes the concrete case of praxis under a given universal of value. But this schema—judgment determined by subsumption, not reflection—is obviously inappropriate to the situation of moral insight. This is the decisive charge against the kind of being that the realm of value possesses: normative power does not accrue to it in the universality of phenomenological intuition but in a concretization appropriate to the situation, one that always finds the agent in the midst of doing something and from there determines appropriate behavior. Value blindness is thus only one side in the unfolding of the problem of value, a side that is obviously conceived on the model of perception and seeing. The determinateness of the agent's situation represents the other side, which has as its consequence not so much blindness as the perspectival character of sight. Like Nicolai Hartmann, Max Scheler tried to take this side into account phenomenologically in understanding determinateness itself as a value, the value of the situation, which then deserves equal consideration with all other values and underlies the universal presuppositions of phenomenological insight into value. It is clear how the moral praxis bound to ethos sees itself as being thereby displaced into a realm of values that offers itself like the stars in the heavens to the moral observer.

Scheler criticized just this in Hartmann's ethics: namely, that it neglected the problem of the moral life of the subject.

> I must entirely repudiate a heaven of ideas and values purportedly subsisting completely "independent" from the nature and possible perfection of living acts of spirit—"independent" not only of human being and human consciousness but from the nature and action of a living spirit—driven out in principle from the domain of philosophy.[9]

But when he himself reflects on the relation of living ethos to insight into the a priori order of values, he remains either stuck in declamation ("Finally, ethics is 'damned bloody stuff,' and if it gives me no directions about how 'I' should be and live in this social and historical context—well, what is it good for?" [manuscript reading, rejected in print]), or he returns precisely to Hartmann's starry sky ("Perhaps with time he slowly achieves that 'pallet of overturned paint pots' [as Scheler had previously described relativity of values]—seen from an appropriate distance and with appropriate understanding—the meaningful integration of a grandiose painting—or at least a fragment of one—in which one can see humanity, colorfully articulated, like a realm of objective values, living independent of it and its formations, living, feeling, and acting, as this shows the history of knowledge to the example of the heavens"). When he adds the remark, "What I have said is meant only as an image, since otherwise only goods, not values can be compared with the stars," he does Hartmann a fundamental injustice, insofar as the latter views the "maieutic" function of ethics as developing and refining consciousness of value. Quite independent of the fact that he actually enunciates a concrete ethos, namely that of fullness, he becomes entangled in the insuperable aporias that open up between moral knowledge and the normative power of ethos. With the idea of research, infinite progress of insight into value is even implied necessarily— unfortunately enough.

Max Scheler tried to help out, supposedly, by viewing the relativity of our concrete insight into value expressed in the variousness of morality as grounded in the necessary mutability of "situational value," whereas philosophical ethics concerns itself with values that are universally valid. This outcome does not suffice. Even Scheler had shown how morals can reverse the a priori ranking of values. The value relationships between the so-called universal values—those which are not primarily mere situational values—constitute the variousness of morals. So he cannot avoid the claim, though somewhat absurd, that a philosophically justified knowledge of moral value must entail a higher ethos.

That Scheler is not actually concerned primarily with a priori insights into value and that these allegedly a priori insights express a concrete ethos become manifest in the almost grotesquely distorted way he depicts Kant's ethics of duty. What a marvelous range of obvious insights he offers against a straw man fashioned by himself! They are all insights into value that in fact subserve a particular ethos (which, viewed from a cultural and sociological perspective, belongs alongside the youth movement's critique of bourgeois merit-based society).

So the whole underlying idea of an order of values susceptible to a priori intuition, along with the metaphysical teleology dependent on it, remains uniquely ambiguous. Nicolai Hartmann went so far as to conceive the order of values as a continuation of the realm of categories whose power to determine reality decreases with higher grades of complexion in any case. On this view, values no longer have any determinative power at all; they are instead related to the power to motivate human beings. This bold thought pushes objectivism—of the categories as well as of "values"—to a climax.

On the other hand, it seems logical to take into account the fact that human reason is determined by actual ethos. This was the wisdom implicit in the idea of "practical philosophy" as Aristotle had founded it and integrated it into the higher totality of "politics." Connecting philosophy and practical reality would remain an insoluble problem if an a priori order of values, considered the basis of all forms of virtue and hierarchies of goodness, were made the object of ethics. Ethics can be nothing but the mere self-clarification of the determinations of concrete ethos. Here Aristotle maintains his position against Socrates. Arete is not Logos but rather μετὰ λόγου. It is not (universally valid) knowledge but rather insight that determines moral behavior. But insight is not the capacity for theoretical knowing; it itself derives from a morally determinate being. It is "reasonableness" (*phronesis*). It makes possible the originary illumination of the particular situation that demands a decision. A situation is not a case of something obeying a theoretical law and being determined by it; it is something that surrounds one and opens itself up only from a practical perspective; everything depends upon one's coming to a decision in the particular formation of one's own moral being (*hexis*). The "universality" of values, susceptible to being intuited in free, situationless "a priori knowledge," cannot achieve givenness for such "practical" insight.

It is no objection that practical philosophy in Aristotle's sense presupposes a fixed, comprehensive ethical gestalt—the one that he himself found retrospectively in the ancient polis, at the moment of its political decline, and now insists is the norm of social life. This is true, but it is always the case that practical "philosophy" arises out of our practically determined being and refers back to it. It nevertheless claims to comprehend the "correct" ethos in its frame-giving structures.

By contrast, the zero degree of being formed by a binding ethos—which is the only way to do justice to the concept of value and its claim to ontological absoluteness—is an illusory phantasm of theoretical reason. Herein lies the limit, but also the legitimacy, of all "practical philosophy": namely, that it does not claim to raise us to the point where we can freely survey an overarching heaven of values; rather, it exposes the supposed search for such a thing as a self-deception that ultimately fails to expand an overly narrow ethos and instead disavows and subverts ethos entirely.

5

Thinking as Redemption:
Plotinus between Plato
and Augustine (1980)

Plotinus does not belong among the giants of philosophical thought whom everybody is always discussing. He cannot be named in the same breath as the great Greek thinkers cast in the mold of Heraclitus, Socrates, Plato, and Aristotle, or with Christian thinkers like Augustine or Thomas, or even with modern thinkers of the quality of Descartes, Leibniz, Kant, or Hegel. He was a Greek thinker of late antiquity and taught philosophy in the Rome of the Caesars—that is, in a Latin-speaking world, though Greek was the language of culture. In this respect alone, this seems a strange constellation for a thinker, especially when one learns that he conceived of himself not at all as purveying new truths but as recuperating Plato's thought. So it must be asked whether he belongs at all in the forefront of our estimation, and if so many count him as belonging there, why we should do so.

We call him a Neoplatonist, which certainly does not mean he was only one among many of the same rank; on the contrary, he stands as Neoplatonism's most important representative. His work has come down to us in complete form; moreover, we have exact, well-authenticated information concerning him and his life, as for no other thinker of antiquity—if we except Socrates, whose portrait was drawn by Plato and other friends and students. Our knowledge of Plotinus is owing to the biography of his student Porphyry that has preserved it for us.

But this situation is in fact not just an accident of tradition. Of course, in philosophy it does seem that tradition is very unfair in distributing its favors. It is indicative, to go no further, that we know almost nothing of Democritus, the great contemporary of Socrates and founder of ancient atomic theory, so consequential in modernity. It was the decisive influence of Plato and Aristotle on late antiquity to which we owe their texts' being handed down.

If the Epicureanism of late antiquity had dominated the time that followed, the work of Democritus—purportedly comprehending some hundred volumes—might have been preserved, and not that of Plato and Aristotle. Now it may well be that the undeciphered papyri of Herculaneum from the library of an Epicurean who was undoubtedly an admirer of Democritus may still hold surprises that could one day revise our image of Greek inquiry into nature. But that would be an accident. It would be preserved like remains or a ruin. Tradition, however, is something different. It involves will and deed, not just accident.

Moreover, the great founders of the Stoic school—Zeno, Chrysippus, and Poseidonius—are barely intelligible figures to us; this too shows to what extent fate governs the event of tradition. In truth, it is probably always something other than mere accident that holds sway over historical memory, and this is quite certainly true in the case of Plotinus. A philosopher in imperial Rome, the capital of the world, who did not live and teach in what had been the site of philosophical schools from time immemorial—I mean Athens—what could be the significance of such a man in his time? What significance could he have had in a world declining toward its end? Concerning his life, we know that he enjoyed close friendship with members of the Caesarean court and the highest circles of Roman aristocracy. Apparently it was the charisma of his noble character that gave him such prestige. But his continuing reputation through the centuries is owing to another circumstance. Plato is called an "anima naturaliter christiana," a soul that was Christian by nature. This description fits Plotinus even more justly, for in his whole human and spiritual demeanor he reflected the temperament of late antiquity and the early centuries of the Christian world: longing for the otherworldly, refinement of the senses and the spirit, flight from the world, and religious enthusiasm. These were centuries in which the ancient religious traditions linked to the names of Pythagoras and Plato unleashed fantastic religious movements; magic, oracular beings, wonder-working, and astrology found receptive souls. We speak of neo-Pythagoreans and Neoplatonists when we are thinking of such wonder-workers and itinerant preachers. Plotinus, however, was quite another breed of man. He was no mystagogue, but a deeply reflective, serious thinker who had absorbed the whole great tradition of Greek philosophy and who, in the name of Plato and under his influence, was able to give thoughtful conceptual expression to the epoch's need for redemption.

But what really raised him to secular eminence was the circumstance that his writings became accessible to early Christian thought through, among others, the translation of Marius Victorinus. This meant much more than that the Greek heritage taken over by the Christian church was enriched by the addition of a significant thinker of the late period. It meant that the church fathers read the great Greek classics of philosophy, especially Plato, with the eyes of Plotinus. From Augustine on, we meet with the influence of Plotinus every step of the way. Obviously it was not so much the memory of his noble character, the trace of his life, as the work he left behind, the trace of his thought, that transmitted the Greek heritage and gave him such lasting impact. Moreover, his influence was not limited to the time of the early church and the development of Christian dogma. The hour of Plotinus came round again at the beginnings of modernity, in the age of humanism. Then humanists sought to free themselves from the straits of church orthodoxy with the help of Greek thought, and for this purpose Plotinus, who mediated classical Greek thought to the early church, was once again the right mediator. Marsilius Ficinus translated him into classical Latin. That was in the fifteenth century.

The thought of Plotinus, moreover, shaped the entire tradition of Platonism from then until very recent times. What dissolved this Platonic-Plotinic unity was the emergence of historical consciousness and the development of the historical sense in the nineteenth century. The new term "Neoplatonism" is a telling expression of the fact that now, for the first time, an essential distinction between Plato and Plotinus was recognized. Even Hegel, the discoverer of the late Platonic dialogues and the one who truly brought the great Greek tradition of metaphysics to completion, still manifests the full influence of Plotinus. He viewed the Neoplatonic movement, as he too called it, as the high point of Greek thought. With Plotinus, Greek thought was brought almost to the verge of Christian truth. This was soon reflected in the Christian theology of the nineteenth century. It had to come into conflict with Hegel's speculative claim to have raised the truth of Christendom and the mystery of the Trinity to the state of the concept. At that time Plotinus and Hegel were grouped together under the rubric of "philosophical gnosis" (Ferdinand Christian Bauer).[1] "Gnosis" just means knowledge, but within Christian theology the concept of gnosis meant the false doctrine that man can bring about his salvation from mortality and fallenness by means of his own striving for knowledge and elevation to divine truths. This was a direct challenge to a revealed religion such as Christianity, and this circumstance raised the thought of Plotinus to world-historical significance even from a religious standpoint.

But more than this, the great philosophical synthesis, made influential by Hegel, that was realized in the work of Plotinus and his successors inspired German Idealism from Fichte to Hegel to build its immense systems. It is not without reason that Kantian and neo-Kantian critics alike of speculative philosophy have combated it precisely as Neoplatonism. But even if we completely disregard these connections to the history of ideas, and to the German philosophical tradition in particular, if we apply ourselves to a direct reading of Plotinus's writings and the tradition concerning his life, we are strangely and deeply moved. What a unique, introspective tone resounds in the play of meditative reflection that informs Plotinus's writings. The person who speaks therein is a teacher, to be sure, but a teacher who is understood along with his auditors and students as being in a common spiritual ecstasy. Even the reader of today encounters this tone like a secret message to the soul. There are still readers nowadays who read Plotinus like holy scripture. Plotinus stands in lonely greatness. We know of many contemporary texts that closely approximate Plotinus's thought, and we possess a highly learned commentary on Aristotle that continually compares him with Plotinus. But what impersonal writers these are—schoolmasters, dogmaticians, formalists, and those who wriggle in a learned conceptual web, where they argue cunningly or demonstrate their great learning. Plotinus is completely different. To be sure, he is not without conceptual subtlety and a tinge of scholasticism. His language is formed by the great tradition of Plato, Aristotle, and the Stoa, and hence is not without learned presuppositions. But Plotinus has so personally appropriated and fully engaged himself in the conceptual schemata with which the age otherwise plagued itself that he stands out as completely unique. He is a genuine phenomenon.

In the age of historical enlightenment, one might have viewed the religious spiritualism and flight from reality that color the thought of this great thinker in a merely historical manner—that is, as an expression of the mood of that period in late antiquity, a mood that came to cloud the rational clarity of the Greek spirit like fog, preceding the rising star of the Christian gospel. Today we view the matter otherwise. We have no desire to deny that the religious enthusiasm of this period cropped out everywhere and that the thinker Plotinus was in its grip as well. But we cannot simply accept the presupposition that as a consequence of this religious turn something new came about, something alien, something foreign to classical Greek thought. To us, the relation of philosophical thought to religious tradition does not seem susceptible of being described in such a simple antithesis. Rather, we view the Greek enlightenment, despite all the cleverness and radicality of its intellectual undertakings, as continually standing in a relation of reciprocity to Greek religion. The great drama of Greek literature displays poetry and philosophy wrestling from early on like two great contenders for the prize of depicting and representing the genuine religious experience of the Greek world.

At the beginning of our century, Homeric theology could still be read as the most ancient source of religious pronouncements. Today we view it far more as a poetic rendition of religion, where a good deal of clarity and rationality, conscious systematization, and critical dismissal of the mystical are brought to bear on the religious tradition as it is transformed into a poetic message. We are filled with wonder at the daring with which the Ionians posed the first great questions about the beginning of everything—about true being and the nonbeing of the nothing, about the systematic balance that governs all human and cosmic events—and how they overcame the religious anthropomorphism of Homeric mythology. But at the same time we see that continuous reinterpretation of the mythic tradition and tidings of the divine went hand in hand with the enlightenment impulse of Greek thought. One need only recall the "philosophy in the tragic age of the Greeks" that had such a direct connection to the "birth of tragedy." This was the vision that Nietzsche, inspired by Wagner, protested. It was the picture not so much of a lost paradise as a paradise of lostness in which Greek pessimism was represented to itself in poetry and thought. But it was not the case, as Nietzsche believed, that Plato's false moral optimism ushered in the end of this great epoch. Today we see that Plato did not ruin the evil Socrates—to avail myself of Nietzsche's famous phrase. Rather, following Socrates, Plato and Aristotle thought through the rational heritage of the Greek spirit to the extreme of radical enlightenment and reunited it with the profound truths of their culture's religious tradition. Enlightenment and tradition achieved a new productive equilibrium. Plato's myths of the soul and its fate, and of the rule of the gods over the course of the world, illustrate this unity through their baroque mixture of styles, where the festiveness of sacred language is wedded to the Ionic spirit of reflection.

The knowledge gained in achieving this new equilibrium was the teleological cosmos that Aristotle described. In it human beings, as the creatures situated closest to the divine, occupy a special place, but they nevertheless remain integrated into the whole cosmic order. At the apex of the ontological order of the universe stand the eternal constellations whose immutable being, like a guarantee and a model of human thought and knowledge, shines over the tumultuous chaos of human things. A highly developed astronomy—which in the guise of the Ptolemaic system retained its validity for many centuries until it was dissolved by Copernicus, the daring canon of Thorn—ultimately remained consonant with the spirit of Greek popular religion. Thus, after presenting the most modern astronomical system of his time, Aristotle wrote that his forefathers and predecessors held the preeminent being of the constellations to be divine. Then he continues (*Met.* Λ 8, 1074b9 ff.):

> One might consider this assertion itself divine. For if one must suppose that every art and kind of knowledge is found many times—if at all—and then sinks back again, one would have to believe that such doctrines are actually vestiges of an ancient knowledge that has survived until the present day. In any case, the faith of the fathers and the early time is only to that extent intelligible.

Thus says Aristotle, the sober-minded master of concepts!

If we consider this tradition of religiously grounded thought, we come to see that it was no artificial revision or distortion that allowed Plotinus, this thinker of late antiquity, to view Plato as both his intellectual and religious model. Philosophy and religion shared common ground throughout the whole history of Greek rationality. When a Stoic thinker like Cleanthes directs his famous hymn to the highest god, he thereby expresses just as much the truth of his own thought as the truth of the myth. If Epicurus and his Roman disseminator Lucretius tried to use subtle logical precision to subvert fear of the gods and of death, nevertheless Lucretius the Epicurean introduced his enlightenment pronouncements with a hymn to a goddess, Aphrodite-Venus. In this way even ancient atheism reconciled itself with the genres honoring the divine powers ruling all ancient life.

Of Plotinus one must say that in an epoch of high religious enthusiasm he was both at the same time: a religious man and a real thinker. Plotinus too had his Socrates, one who had awakened him philosophically: Ammonius the sack-bearer, who apparently lived a very unpretentious and frugal life—hence his nickname. Ammonius was perfectly familiar with Plato, but never wrote a line. Plotinus was among his most ardent students, and followed him so assiduously that it was not until very late that he decided to write down the meditations with which he created his own circle of students in Rome. Thanks to the faithfulness of Porphyry, we have his whole corpus, all the lectures, which are like conversations with himself: putting questions, breaking off, starting up again, raising objections, and spinning out the most subtle dialectic—until at the end there comes not so much a solution, an answer, or result, but instead a speculative voice and a vision bathed in light. Of course, one needs to have reached the heights of Greek philosophical culture in order to follow these dialectical subtleties at all. Yet, again and again brilliant images and metaphors betray the visionary power of this thinker, once again transforming the entirety of the Greek philosophical tradition into original thought.

Doubtless Plotinus seized upon Platonic motifs again and again, transforming them with penetrating dialectic. That beyond the multiplicity of Ideas thinking inquires after the One, which, as the Good and the Beautiful itself, like an origin from afar, transcends and grounds the world of ideas, this whole realm of true being—this was Plato's teaching too. But in his dialogues Plato avoids making any precise statement concerning the One, or the Good that is necessarily only one but also many as well. He leaves completely open how the Idea relates to the multiplicity of appearances, and especially how the Good and the Beautiful relate to everything that is good and beautiful, and how exactly the sensory world participates in the intelligible world of Ideas. The opposition between that world and this one has an almost religious significance for him. But the contrast of these worlds to one another is hardly as flat and simple as the so-called two worlds theory of Platonism would have it. Admittedly, the question about the sense in which the Good can be the "cause" or ground of being almost dissolves in the sense that the Good and the Beautiful are always immanent in existents. But, unlike Plato, Plotinus devotes the entire weight of his thought to prescinding the One entirely from all defining determinations and even completely dissociating it from "thought"; for by its nature thought cannot be the One, because it falls apart into the duality of thinking and thought. The negative path that he pursues in thinking of the One makes Plotinus the father of negative theology, progenitor of the so-called *via negativa*. Thought can come to grips with the eminence of the divine only by transcribing it in terms of universal negation. This is the Neoplatonic theology which interpreted the first "hypothesis" of Plato's *Parmenides* as a document of negative theology in the same sense.[2]

The fundamental problem to which Plotinus always returns is the necessity, and the impossibility, of thinking the One. The nous, the thought that thinks itself, which Aristotle had used to describe the mode of being of the divine, is inadequate. Instead, we must get beyond the duality of thinking. The One which is the Good and the Beautiful first comes to exist in the union and fusion of the thinking and the thought. This transcendence of the One, however, means at the same time the highest immanence of all beings in the One. Even where a being is not a thinking being, the unity of the One manifests itself in everything that is and is one. Thus the teleological cosmos of Aristotle is transformed into a dynamically pervasive All.

For Plato and Aristotle, too, life and vitality self-evidently constituted the fundamental nature of the divine, as of the totality of the world. But in order to explain the ordered movement of the cosmos, Plato—this Pythagorean mathematician

—had recourse to mythic fables. A demiurge ordered the whole according to inviolable harmonies. Moreover, sober Aristotle, who had his eye more on life than on the mathematical, conceived of an order of movement kept in motion by the unmoved mover's mysterious power of attraction, as by a mechanics of love. Plotinus, by contrast, puts the vitality of the living into effect in a new sense. This is primarily the concept of δύναμις, the "power and possibility" to which Plotinus gives a new accent and a kind of ontological primacy. Of course, δύναμις is essentially related to ἐνέργεια, possibility and reality. Such had been the basic doctrine of Aristotle's metaphysics. But in the Hellenic age, the Platonic-Aristotelian concept of being —in which the Eleatic heritage lived on and "being" meant what was present in thought—acquired a new, dynamic corollary meaning: not presence, but the power that maintains and expresses itself. Power, however, is always living power—not power that expends itself in expression and is weakened thereby. Living power fulfills itself and maintains itself by the power of its activity. We can also speak of power that overflows itself, as we see in the case of the exuberance of life that overflows itself in drama and dance. This is something we need to fathom in its whole ontological meaning. The Stoa had already considered this new concept of power, of breath and tension, in a preparatory way. They paved the way for a new turn in the thought of being. No longer is being the streaming present that is manifest to the gaze of thought only in its predictability—as idea, nature, substance; being is now the secret power that is dormant in everything, a being that never lets itself be seen, assayed, or exhausted, but manifests itself only in its expressions.

Clearly, the idea of a creator of all—which for Plato had been largely a philosophical metaphor of the rational structure of the world—acquires more reality from such a concept of being. The well-known expression of the new understanding of being that the Neoplatonists project into Plato is the concept of "emanation," the outflow or overflow of an inexhaustible spring.[3] This is what holds together the great architectonics of the world. These waters pervade all—from the One that is beyond, to the world of spirits and the world of mind, to the soul that experiences itself, to the organic formative power of nature.

Listen to a sample of this meditative mode of argument:

> The One, however, must be the origin of and prior to the whole, so that through it the whole can come to be. Even if it were each single existent, each would first of all be identical to every other, and then everything would all be the same, namely all in one, and differences would cease. From this follows that it is no part of the whole but prior to the whole. What is it, then? It is the power of the whole, without whose existence the whole itself could not be, nor the spirit, which is the principle and whole of life. What is thus superior to life is the origin of life. For the enactment of life, which is the whole, cannot at all be the principle. Rather, it has itself emerged as from a spring. Think, for example, of a spring which has no other origin and is itself the origin of all streams, which is never exhausted in streaming out but rather continues on within itself, and this in such a way that the streams which flow out of it, before each flows in its own direction, are at one within it—in such a way, however, that each is already cognizant, as it were, whereunto its waters will pour out. Or think about the life of a great tree flowing through it from top to bottom, and this in such a way that it remains an origin in itself, without dissipating itself in cours-

ing through the whole, as if it had its real place in the root. This origin gives the tree its life in all its fullness and yet remains in itself and is not many but rather the origin of many. This is nothing to wonder at. Or rather it is astonishing. (*Enneads* iii, 8 (30), 9, 50–10, 14)

As you can see, Plotinus loves metaphors for the organic unity of effect and of life. The image of a spring is always nearest to hand for him. Also filling his vision is the powerful circulation of a tree with its roots sinking into the depths of the earth and rising high into the sky, but preeminently the light, this enigmatic everywhere, which may stream out of only one source but at that very instant spreads itself on all sides, illuminating everything in its light, harboring all beings with its light and comprehending everything that is. It may become lost in the indeterminable darkness where nothing is, but its reflection shines back from every being.

Those familiar with Rilke will immediately realize that a Plotinic spirit inspired the angelic vision of the *Duino Elegies*.

Frühe Geglückte, ihr Verwöhnte der Schöpfung.
Höhenzuge, morgenrötliche Grate
aller Erschaffung, — Pollen der blühenden Gottheit,
Gelenke des Lichtes, Gänge, Treppen, Throne,
Räume aus Wesen, Schilde aus Wonne, Tumulte
stürmisch enzuckten Gefühls und plötzlich, einzeln,
Spiegel, die die entströmte eigene Schönheit
wiederschöpfen zurück in das eigene Antlitz.[4]

This is the other direction of the cosmic drama of emanation and overflow: the return. Here being first becomes true being: just as the angels are the truer beings because their feeling returns to itself.

The Un-Platonic motif of ascending to the One takes on a new form when the visionary power of Plotinus conjures up the spirit world, which, divorced from the sensory world, gives promise to the inquiring soul of rising up and glimpsing the foundation of the cosmos. It is like a great cosmic drama from which the spiritual path of thought takes its coordinates. The rise from the sensory to the spiritual, and beyond the multiplicity of the spiritual world to the One, the Good, and the Beautiful, is completely within the spirit of Plato. But this rise is a return, the path of the soul's reversal. What precedes it is a great world event, the emanation of the soul and the whole multiplicity of beings from the original unity: an inconceivable process of effluence, emanation, like an act of mere forwardness from which is created the multifarious cosmos of forms released into being. This order of things is ruled by the law of near and far with respect to the One. Like a source of light that is lost in the thick darkness of the night, but as long as it is not entirely swallowed up by the darkness, it lets appear what is reached by the beams streaming out from it, most brightly and clearly what is nearest, and what is furthest most dimly—this is how Plotinus describes the great cosmic process in which the lost and longing soul of the individual tries to find a home for its own errant Dasein. This insight into the great cosmic drama brought about by philosophy's sinking down into meditation at the same time leads the soul thrown into being back to the living ground of the One.

The Christian concept of gnosis can be justly applied to this thinking. Yet it is not through the revelation of an otherworldly God, but through the deepening and spiritualization of one's own earthly human being that the path of redemption opens up. The great spiritual breath that raises the lost soul to mystical union with the ultimate ground blows through the whole. The insightful sinking into the One, the "unio mystica," designates only the final stage of the return. The metaphysics of Plotinus is a doctrine of being as that which returns by turning back to its origin.

We hear the language of Christian mysticism. We recall the phrase of Meister Eckhart: " 'Why are you going out?' 'To find my way home'."

6

Myth in the Age of Science (1981)

1. The Rediscovery of Mythology by Historical Thought

The story of myth's reawakening claim to religious validity is well known. After Vico and Herder served as forerunners, the Romantic movement in particular turned its critique on the rationalism of the Enlightenment and its "sad atheistic twilight" (Goethe) in recognition of the religious significance of myths. At the same time the mythic luminosity possessed by the holy story of Christianity acquired new brilliance. A new feeling for the mythical is discernible in the poetic creations of the age, whether in Novalis and his many friends and followers who extolled the Christian epoch, in the rediscovery of Dante, or in Hölderlin's poetic revival of the world of the Greek gods, which "the individual" enters through reconciliation.[1]

Of course, in the realm of poetry, as in the plastic arts, pagan mythology had long since won the right to exist alongside biblical materials. Christian humanism came to be realized in this patent unity of effect. The concept of allegory even permitted the incorporation of both teachings about the heathen gods and heroic tales from Christian culture, without impugning the indubitable superiority of the Christian world view. But now, given the new self-awareness of the Age of Reason, a new problem arose in the context of the famous "querelle des anciens et des modernes" about that patency and indubitability. The "querelle" had begun by accepting the humanist model, which now had to reach a compromise not just with Christendom; it came into conflict with the Enlightenment's pride in progress—a literary feud, no doubt. But what emerged in resolving this literary conflict was something fundamentally new: the historical mode of thought. This could not happen without increasing the religious value of heathen mythology.

Hume's skeptical critique of metaphysics, and the historical perspective which underlay his *Natural History of Religion*, worked in the same direction. Contemporary metaphysics had tried to construct its systems so as to mediate between the traditional metaphysics of the church and the idea of modern science. Now, at the peak of the Enlightenment, the empirical view of science fused with the slowly awakening idea of history.

After Vico's lonely emergence, it was primarily the science of classical antiquity (*Altertumswissenschaft*) that discovered the mythic world view of antiquity proper. To be sure, this did not occur without everything being viewed in relation to Christian revelation. Thus it happened that Lowth, the English preromantic, called the Old Testament "holy poesy," holding it to be the crowning perfection of poetic mythology. This had great influence in Germany and especially in Göttingen. We have a theologically oriented book[2] to thank for our knowledge that the rebirth of myth in Germany is due primarily to Heyne, the Göttingen philologist. He took the decisive step by no longer speaking of "mythic poesy," but rather recognizing in myth a genuinely religious experience. Sitting at the feet of Heyne in Göttingen then were the two Schlegels, Friedrich Creuzer, Friedrich August Wolf, Johann Heinrich Voß, and Wilhelm von Humboldt. Heyne called Herder his "dear friend" (though Herder may have been more an enthusiastic disseminator than an original discoverer of the world of mythic experience). We need not only view Heyne as indeed the mediator of English preromanticism to German scholarship, but also acknowledge that he was the great teacher of the history of myth, who brought the word "myth" into new esteem. He founded a whole "mythic school," and the effect of Göttingen philology reached far beyond biblical scholarship. The *sermo mythicus* which the "mythic school" was then trying to investigate is no longer viewed in an aesthetic or literary way. In this respect the "mythic school" went far beyond the English preromanticism of a Lowth. In mythic discourse it discerned the language of the childhood of the human race, preceding all poetic, and especially all written, modes of discourse. It is here that the grand visions of Vico first found acceptance. With them Heyne established the main lines of the scholarly approach to myths that endured for a long time. Myth precedes all direct tradition. From its being founded anthropologically in the childhood of the human race, mythic discourse acquired its historical rights, and from then on it affirmed its own proper status alongside philosophical and poetic discourse.

2. Difficulties in the Historical Reconstruction of Myth

To be sure, such mythical ur-knowledge presents special difficulties to historical research. What it has to do is to reconstruct a tradition that is not at all directly accessible and that, insofar as we know anything about it at all, is penetrated through and through with philosophical and poetic influences. Of its own nature, myth can never be grasped in its original purity. This fact set new tasks for thought, which needed to proceed in different ways along the most varied paths of modern science: for the philosopher differently from the theologian, and so too for modern research in antiquities. Philosophy had to defend its own claim to the power of reason and the priority of the concept, and it was able to take cognizance of mythic consciousness only as an undeveloped form of truth. In this way it came simultaneously into competition with Christian theology, which insisted on the absolute claim of Christian revelation and on sublating the religious truth of the mythic into itself, insofar as it recognized it. And, finally, in competition with comparative study of religion, historical and critical research had to find out how historical methods could be applied to something which to be sure was its object—the original content of mythic experience—but which was transmitted only in literary form, which means in poetic structures and meaning. Thus, at least, the subject must have appeared to a scientific consciousness that acknowledged no other "facts" than the facts of faith concerning holy history on the one hand and the scientific concept of fact on the other.

3. Myth and Philosophy

It is obvious that the teleological schema of ancient biblical history retained its validity even in the age of the attempted synthesis of religion and philosophy, which was supposed to give ultimate shape to modern metaphysics. The speculative philosophers had to subordinate myth to concept, whether because they viewed it as a sensory preliminary to Christian revelation or just as a sensory preliminary to the speculative reconciliation of image and concept, religion and philosophy, as in Hegel's system. Hegel's solution was that of Christian spiritualism. He interpreted the holy advent in which God became man, the death on the cross, and the resurrection by way of the structure of "Geist," which continually returns from alienation and being other to being itself. In this way, not only every mythic event, but also God's unique act of grace is sublated into the conceptual necessity of thought and Geist.

Schelling's own claim did not go quite so far. Yet he too viewed the future religion to which philosophical religion aspired as the perfect experience of God. In contrast to Hegel, his *Philosophie der Mythologie und der Offenbarung* was still a "positive" philosophy. That is, in both he saw not the necessity of the concept but historical freedom at work. For him the development of polytheism as well as Christian revelation, where it is overcome, are stages of one process. "The ideas whose succession immediately gave rise to . . . polytheism are produced in consciousness without its doing anything, even against its will."[3] The point of such a philosophy of mythology is this: in myth no further invention whatever is at work. The philosophical insight represented by Schelling frees myth from the "poetic viewpoint" and gives it back its full religious significance. Every distinction between content and form, substance and its dress, doctrine and history, misunderstands the reality of the theogonic process, "which is prescribed by an essential relation of the human consciousness and God."[4]

This is the heritage of romanticism: namely, that since then, the word and concept of myth have been endowed with new significance. The mythic offers a new concept of value. Josef Görres' *Mythengeschichte der alten Welt* and Creuzer's *Symbolik* were the first scholarly fruits of romantic thought, though of course they soon fell prey to the critique consequent on subsequent historical research. In addition to "myth" the word *mythos* (*Mythe*—a term probably connected to "fabula" in Latin and French) was also used primarily by poets—up until Uhland. The call for a new mythology, a popular religion, was heard everywhere. The generation of Schelling, Hegel, and Hölderlin shared it from the bottom up, and it was obvious that the ancient world served as a model for this call and this demand. Not just classical antiquity, however, but also other traditions, Oriental, Islamic, and Indian, pointed in the same direction. Of course, a new aesthetic mythology—one that was both to be a mythology of reason and to unite the intellectual and sensory side of religion—had to remain merely programmatic. The so-called *Systemprogramm* that formulated this ideal and that was certainly private work of the moment—whoever the author might be—did express a real need of the time. The myth of socialism (Saint-Simon), the myth of power (Sorel), and other political ideologies that wear a religious nimbus go some way toward confirming this. So too all the ways in which Germanic mythology was revitalized and reworked by art and its purveyors, Richard Wagner as well as Nietzsche, represent far-reaching instances of such old/new mythology.

With the mention of Nietzsche, the topic of "myth and science" enters a whole new dimension. Since then, the use of the word and the conceptual resonance that it possesses have been determined, as it were, by two antithetical poles, formed by two different derivations of the word *mythos*. The word *mythological* has a predominantly negative meaning. For theologians the "mythological" is that which can claim no validity in the face of the gospel's truth claim; and for historians it is what cannot stand up to the concept of fact and reality basic to modern science. *Mythic*, by contrast, has a completely different resonance. It awakens not only the vision of a greatness unknown in the experience of the present world, something beyond experience that happened within the real world, yet leaves all experience behind it—for instance, great deeds, victories, events that are on all tongues and thus have a continuing life. In a still more comprehensive sense, "mythic" also means everything that preserves the underlying substance of a living culture. Nietzsche has more to say about the abuse than the use of history for life.

Such a view of myth is fatally ambiguous when it is connected, as for Nietzsche, with the esteem for the new myth that Richard Wagner represents for him and who in Nietzsche's vision was to renew Greek tragic art in our century. What makes the ambiguity involved in the concept of the mythic so fatal is the fact that giving birth to a new myth was a conscious aim, especially in the case of the theatrical genius, Wagner. With this step, myth forfeits the spontaneity and validity that belonged to its early period. This becomes clear if we consider the Führer cults of totalitarian states and—still more uncanny—the enigma of brainwashing. Only a scientifically superstitious consciousness could reduce such "turnabouts" to chemical effects. The "dialectic of enlightenment" hits upon the truth of the matter.

4. Scientific Research into Myth

Ultimately the topic "myth and science" is forced to ask in what sense there can be a science of myth. The background common to all historical approaches to the essence of myth is psychology. As a result of the modern Enlightenment, all inquiry into myth bases it in a fact of consciousness: namely, the imagination that creates myths. Insofar as we can discern a common element in the research of the nineteenth and twentieth centuries, it is that there is no longer any question about the truth of myth, and that therefore explanation of mythic consciousness, in the form of a rational explanation of myths, can claim no validity. By and large we can divide nineteenth-century myth research into two main streams. On one side was comparative theology. At the time, this appeared to be the sole and universal method of entering this realm, and it drew into its train the historical human sciences of the classical kind as well. For comparative theology, classical antiquity represented merely a particular case within a larger whole. On the other side was the classical science of antiquity (*Altertumswissenschaft*), whose tradition of thorough research greeted every constructive interpretation of mythic tradition with necessary historical skepticism. In our century, however, both basic tendencies of research into myth received new interest.

Given its Christian background, modern science, and in particular modern science of antiquity, viewed the literary tradition—epic and other genres of poetry that contain echoes of the mythic—as offering no legitimate access to original mythic consciousness. "Poets lie too much." This at least was the view of nineteenth-century historical research, like Plato's though steeped in the Christian concepts of faith and knowledge. Under these conditions the two aspects of tradition acquired a methodological preeminence. On one side there was language, this prehistory of the human spirit, which promised to get behind all the literary reformulations deriving from poetic imagination; and on the other side were the remains of rituals actually practiced that have come down to us in many forms: sites, customs, festivals. Thanks to the power of self-preservation that such customs have, they reach back much farther than all literary tradition.

Thus comparative theology was in large part constructed on the model of comparative linguistics. The common linguistic elements in the religious vocabulary of Indo-European peoples seemed to one Max Müller to be the comprehensible basis for reconstructing the primordial religious experience common to these peoples, and soon ethnographic research was expected to draw new conclusions about the mores and customs and religious worlds of other cultures. Within research into religious language, the names of the gods exercised a special fascination. In Hermann Usener they emerged entirely into the foreground. For him they represented the final result, as it were, of the gods taking on form. Scholars trained in theology explained the primordial religious experience behind these names as an act of primordial name-giving in the suddenness of the inspired moment. On the basis of such "special gods," the system of religious concepts was formed. It could not be ignored that there was one charge that could brought against such a theory: "No one prays to concepts." This was the charge that Wilamowitz in particular raised against Usener's theory of special gods.

Wilamowitz himself synthesized his immense research into the history of myth in the grand work of his old age bearing the title *Der Glaube der Hellenen* (The Faith of the Hellenes). Here a conception of faith acquired in Christendom was, quite as a matter of course, projected back onto the dawn of mythic experience. One might well ask whether the Greeks could have at all expressed the titular concept of "faith" in their own language. *Nomos* and νομίζειν might come to mind, if only convention, custom, and law did not take precedence. On the other hand, we might think of *eusebia*,[5] the demeanor of pious respect employed in performing public religious ceremonies. But in both alternatives the real concrete substance of Greek mythic tradition is lacking. This fact cannot be concealed by the immense power of intuition with which the great scholar Wilamowitz traces the concrete facts of landscape and tribal life, historical events, and cultic practices. Here the insuperable limits of historical research come to light. What Wiliamowitz claims to accomplish—namely, to make intelligible the "heartfelt relation" of the Greeks to their gods—cannot succeed on this basis. What he says about the forms of the gods and their transformations does not get beyond the general idea of powers and forces, to which no one can pray either.

This is the point from which Walter F. Otto set out. He examined the poetic formations that we find in Greek literary tradition and tried to take their religious claims seriously.[6] His attempt at interpretation begins not with the powers, but the forms that appear in the great poetry, and in so doing he took up Schelling's insights. Greek polytheism, he argues, is the necessary form of the religious process in which the experience of the divine is articulated. The gods are aspects of reality, a reality which it would be nonsensical to doubt, that have been given shapes amenable to sensory perception in the forms of the Olympian deities. Love as an overpowering passion, the ecstatic self-forgetting of military fervor, lucky ingenuity or cunning, radiant spirituality and serenity—these things that come over humankind like experiences of overweening reality are not rationalistic explanations of traditional divine forms, but descriptions of the experienced reality itself. Even Dionysius, the god of wine and intoxication, is this kind of powerful reality that bewitches and enthralls human beings, and the reality of this power hardly requires justification.

A methodological argument for the religious reality of these divine forms is offered by the fact, mentioned above, that the poetic tradition, in whose light Walter F. Otto and his student Karl Kerényi interpreted this mythic world, led with seamless continuity into the rational world where Greek thought came to be realized. It may occur to us that in the many-colored spectrum of Greek gods which unfolds here, the form of the highest god is missing: Zeus, father of gods and men. This omission can hardly be ascribed to the oversight of a scholar who knew very well that it was precisely the triumph of the Zeus religion that unified the whole family of Olympian gods. The reason is, rather, the almost involuntary effect of the fact that the variety of the universe was comprehended in the great unifying figure of the father-god as in one single powerful reality. This was the point at which the philosophical religion of transcendence could link up and then, in the Hellenistic age, extend the lines of the divine reality toward the One that is beyond. Schelling's conception of theogonic processes here finds a new interpretation. Greek polytheism represents, as it were, a stage on the way to "Geist" and to the truth of the one God.

In recent decades, French structuralism has made a sensation in being applied to mythology. Once again the primacy of language has proved fruitful for understanding myth, but no longer by using individual nomenclature or forms of mythic experience associated with names as clues for reconstructing mythological interconnections. It is now the principle on which language itself is constructed that offers a new analogical method. The path-breaking inquiries of Saussure had shown that the generative power of language makes use of sets of oppositions. Words call forth their counterwords, and thus unfolds the vocabulary of language in a process of construction whose structural regularity represents a constant across all the variety of human language forms. Lévi-Strauss and his friends succeeded in constructing a generative grammar of mythic consciousness, as it were. It allowed them to discern constants and regularities in mythic tradition that hold true like unbreakable laws, despite the arbitrariness due to historical variation or imaginative inventiveness. This presented the possibility of making sense of the forms of mythic clouds no less unexpected than that opened up by the psychology of the unconscious in our century. Freud's analysis of mythic consciousness disclosed amazing regularities in the prehistory of the soul, and the same applies to the archetypes that C. G. Jung discerned as constants in the dream life of our unconscious.

Thus we can speak of a science of myth that goes beyond the romantic heritage of the historical sciences, as far as it has proved possible to rationalize the secret of mythic experience. Once again, however, the insuperable antagonism between myth and science seems to have asserted itself. What is beyond consciousness rises up neither in the one nor in the other direction, but wholly in the consciousness of itself.

How imagination creates myths may have been in part illuminated in these ways, but the forms of art and religion composed from them have lost none of their expressive power thereby. However much light is shed on the dark prehistory of the human soul, the capacity to dream remains its strongest power.

7

The Ethics of Value and
Practical Philosophy (1982)

It is more than half a century since Nicolai Hartmann's *Ethics* appeared, and even longer since I felt the stimulation and challenge that Nicolai Hartmann's personal supervision and friendly guidance aroused in me as a young man. So, for me, a new engagement with his work and the problems of an ethics of value (*Wertethik*) represents a kind of self-examination. "A good head weighs both the gain and the loss."

In the twenties, of course, we students all had a tense relationship with Nicolai Hartmann. Hartmann was very much aware that he was swimming "against the current"—the current of philosophy formed by historical consciousness. This philosophy was just as dissatisfied with the methodologism of the ruling neo-Kantian school as he was; but as far as he was concerned it was stuck in the same circle of self-reflection, in that it was looking for the immediacy of life. "Phenomenology," however, also exercised a strong attraction on us students because of its intuitive elements. For us, as for Nicolai Hartmann, what we meant by phenomenology, to be sure, was more the sweeping insatiability and demonic possession with which Max Scheler followed out his brilliant intuitions than the sincere concern for transcendental self-grounding that Edmund Husserl viewed as his life's work. Yet we young people were in an especially critical situation. After the end of the war, in the years when we were in need of steadiness and orientation, we were exposed to a powerful disintegration of tradition. Its effect on those of us who had been seduced by self-reflection into philosophy was to throw us back entirely upon our own devices. Our demands for a new ground and new standards truly did not represent a demand for the patient work of research.

Now, the ongoing course of events in the twentieth century was held to have thoroughly solidified the dominant position of science and the technocracy based on it (a new word for a new thing) and to have extended the application of science to the field of society, especially after the Second World War. The horrible phantasmagoria of trench warfare in the First World War had already begun to undermine the optimism about progress characteristic of the so-called Wilhelminian or Victorian age. In the realm of philosophy, this toppled epistemology from its prominence. Thus we were attracted by the "resurrection of metaphysics" that was proclaimed at the time. That, of course, could signify a great many things. Against the constructive idealism of the Marburg school, Hartmann's "metaphysics of knowledge" brought new respect to the "being in itself" of things and thereby to the metaphysical tradition that in truth remained tied to Kant's critique. The "thing in itself" found new advocates. This turn away from Idealism was fundamental to Max Scheler's phenomenology as well as Hartmann's connection to it. Moreover, Nicolai Hartmann discovered, despite Husserl's motto of correlation research, a distinction between act-phenomenology and object-phenomenology, and made himself the spokesman for the latter. This manifested itself, for example, in the fact that he took special interest not in Hegel's *Phenomenology of Spirit* but in his *Science of Logic*. Although there is much corresponding to Cohen's logic of origin to be observed in Hartmann's later studies of the theory of categories—which demonstrate the continuity of the idealistic theory of categories from Hegel's logic, to Trendelenburg's critique of Hegel, up to himself—what interested Hartmann in Cohen was not that the latter founded logic in the "judg-ment of origin." Categories "are." From Hartmann we learned as well as we could the play of categories and modalities.

But our own interest was absolutely focused on the practi-cal—that is, ethics. Here Max Scheler was the path-breaker. Of course, Scheler had devoted his gifts for phenomenologi-cal intuition to the revitalization of the Catholic conception of order; thus his material ethics of value (*materiale Wertethik*) de-veloped a kind of hierarchy of values that reached its apex in the infinite person of God and the value of the holy. With the pathos of the researcher and the spirit of a pioneer, Hartmann seized on the brilliant suggestions of Scheler's ethics—but the religious impulse was not what he had in mind.

I have described how the concept of value emerged in nine-teenth-century ethics in a study of my own,[1] in which I praised the role of Hermann Lotze. Now, neither Lotze nor Windel-band, who was his student, was really held in esteem by Scheler or Hartmann. Apparently the latter considered them, not en-tirely unjustly, as being transcendental-idealistic nominalists. In Scheler one can detect a certain amount of Franz Bren-tano's influence—mediated through the young Husserl. Since Alois Roth's publication of Husserl's early thoughts on ethics,[2] there can no longer be any doubt whatever that in this re-spect Scheler followed in Husserl's footsteps. But what is really surprising and paradoxical is the role that Friedrich Nietzsche played for him as well as for Hartmann. It is surprising inso-far as Nietzsche's revolutionary pathos had drawn the concept of value right into the center, while at the same time he made "value" completely relative to "life" or the will to power. Thus he offered no basis whatever for an objectivist apiorism like that represented by Scheler and Hartmann. So both of them read Nietzsche against the grain, as it were, not as the destroyer of old tables of value and creator of new ("Revaluation of All

Values"), who discovered a "beyond" to good and evil; rather, he was esteemed as someone who opened people's eyes to values that had been overlooked or repressed, and thus as a kind of collaborator in value research, especially in the service of a priori philosophy of morality—that is, "material ethics of value."

The paradoxical nature of this estimate of Nietzsche is obvious. It governs Scheler less than it does Hartmann, who paid him homage under the title "Vom Vorbeigehen" (On Passing By). Enlisting Nietzsche in value research might be especially significant today. In our century's call to emancipation and its echo in the life of industrialized society, Nietzsche has actually functioned to open up moral narrowness (which today is being repeated in America).

Just as bold, though less paradoxical, was the fact that Nicolai Hartmann took Aristotle's ethics into consideration in value research. He completely disregarded the "anthropological" grounding of Aristotle's ethics, especially the relation of *physis* and hexis, which are definitive for Aristotle's concept of arete. That he did not recognize Hexis as an expression of the ontological constitution of humanity is shown by the fact that he translated this Greek word as "Verhalten" (attitude). In fact, he understood Aristotle's analysis of the virtues not as a description of *Haltungen* (modes of behavior) but—starting from the consciousness or feeling of value—as an attitude toward "values." Thus Hartmann extended the concept of value even to the problem of concretizing the types of virtue. It is well known that Aristotle accomplishes this task through the "dianoetic" virtue phronesis, and it is represented in the analysis of ethical virtues merely in vague phrases (ὡς δεῖ, ὡς ὁ ὀρθὸς λόγος, ὡς ἂν ὁ φρόνιμος ὁρίσειε: *Nicomachean Ethics* 1106b36 ff.).

Hartmann objectivizes even these phrases and sees in them the value of the situation! His orientation to a realm of values existing in themselves, which for him were a priori givens, emerged with special clarity when he characterized his discovery of the concept of "value synthesis" as a great step forward in insight. For him this was a real discovery of a double star or a constellation in the heaven of values, comparable to the astronomical phenomena which it was Hartmann's passion to observe through a large telescope. Indeed, these value syntheses signify an approximation to the phenomena themselves, as they are really met with in concrete human existence. But Hartmann arrived at them from underneath, as it were—that is, from the abstract givens of value consciousness, which come to appear only as elements within a unified mode of behavior and first exist for us only in this unity. I remember how angry it made him when he happily described the discovery of value syntheses, and I replied in the brazen simplicity of youth: But that is really nothing but Aristotle's arete and its *mesotes* structure. For Hartmann the concept of value (like the concept of categories) was the concept of pure givenness, which needed to be studied in a phenomenological and descriptive way. Later he was also very angry when I invoked Brentano's concept of value in a review of his student Harald Schilling.[3] There, it is true, the a priori givenness of values is never proclaimed in a clear way, and for Hartmann this was the important thing. On the other hand, it cannot be denied that the tradition stemming from Brentano very much influenced Husserl and Scheler. Moreover, Scheler sharply criticized Hartmann's ethics for applying the concept of value to Aristotle.

What was it, then, that left me so unsatisfied with Hartmann's rich and brilliant book on ethics, and how does what Hartmann's incisive study of value strived to open up look today? Basically it is one and the same problem that I have pursued since my beginnings. I first encountered it in the pathos with which Kierkegaard's Christian radicalism attacked all "understanding from a distance," both that of speculative philosophy and that of church theology. It was the motif of existential philosophy (which did not exist at the time) that bound me early on to historicity and the heritage of Dilthey. Thus, of necessity, I became aware of the ambiguity of the task of philosophical ethics.

Philosophy possesses no competence to prescribe and becomes laughable when it tries to take on such a role: this scarcely requires proof. The obligatory nature of a moral system receives its indubitable obviousness from customs in force. To offend against them is not really to contest their validity insofar as every justification attempts to deny that the action really offends against them, or to mitigate or excuse it—and that means recognition of the norms is presupposed. The difference between good and evil, positive and negative, is always constitutive for the sense of moral applicability. Aristotle rightly says that the "principle" to begin with in all deliberation about the good is the "that" (*das "Daß"*), the recognition of the force of the norm. Of course, a "moral principle" cannot subsist without being expressly formed in what we call "upbringing"—realized through modeling, guidance, and instruction. Virtue, however, is not something that can be "learned." Even the much remarked intellectualism of Greek ethics and the Socratic-Platonic paradox of virtue/knowledge only apparently imply that the good can be learned. The paradox of virtue/knowledge is in truth distinct from its self-evident basis in human custom, which is always present in thought and which finds confirmation even in emancipatory enlightenment. Every Greek was continually reminded of this by a famous poem of Theognis:

> To produce and raise a mortal creature is easier,
> than to implant a noble mind in it.
> No one has yet discovered,
> how to make the wild controlled

or a noble person of a wicked one.
If a god had given to the sons of Aescelapius
the art of healing men's wickedness and evil minds,
they would have received
great and large recompense for it.[4]

The poem closes: "But through teaching you will never make a wicked man into a good one." It is not for nothing that Aristotle—who, just like Plato, cited this poem without affirming the ethic of nobility behind it—designated ethos (that is, the state of being arising from training) as the fundamental ground of ethics. Thus, it was he who posed the question about right and the limits of a theoretical approach to ethical questions, and who used the intellectual image of *skopos*, the focus on the target that facilitates the archer's success. In his valuable contribution to revitalizing practical philosophy, J. Ritter[5] mistook this image by associating it with Plato's metaphor of the hunt, without sufficiently realizing that, vis-à-vis the conventionalism of the Sophists, Plato had already given a new foundation to the question of the Good. Aristotle is followed only when he conceptualizes the ethics of the polis without the polis.

My description of the attitude of the generation to which I then belonged makes it understandable that Aristotle's thoroughly incidental self-restriction became connected in our eyes with the critique of "knowing from a distance" that occupied us, especially because it was joined to his critique of Plato's idea of the Good. Kant became another collaborator of mine, in that his *Foundation of the Metaphysics of Morals* contained an explicit justification of the transition from the self-evidence of the moral consciousness to moral philosophy. Here, it seemed to me and still does, is expressed the real justification, not only of moral philosophy, but of all philosophy as such. It consists in this: that for thinking beings the use of reason is always in need of critique. In theorizing it serves to prevent falling prey to the transcendental appearance that seduces one into the errors of metaphysics, and in the moral realm it serves to prevent rationalizing away the universality of the categorical imperative (which I have termed the "dialectic of the exception"[6]). The formalism of Kant's ethics seemed to me well suited to perform this negative, indirect function of philosophical reflection. Gerhard Krüger's fine book *Philosophie und Moral in der Kantischen Kritik*[7] was also of help to me.

It was against the background of these interests that the material ethics of value raised a critical question for me: namely, how philosophical research in value could justify itself in contrast to the normative character of practical reason. My first lecture "On the Concept and History of Greek Ethics" (Marburg, 1928) began with a detailed critique of the ethics of value and directed itself to the question of what normative ethos could be claimed by such a philosophical task as research in the realm of values.

Now, neither Scheler nor Hartmann completely foreclosed this question. For Scheler, as well as for Hartmann, it was obvious that all consciousness of value and all feeling of value are grounded in the life forms of the ethos and its normative validity. Scheler was always interested in the relativity of ethical forms, in both their historical and cultural multiplicity. But he scarcely viewed this multiplicity as limiting the absolutism of the values themselves. Probably he had asked himself what social and historical conditions had freed him from neo-Kantian productive Idealism and from Kant's ethical formalism. He suggests as much when he writes: "It is only after the breakup of the ethics based on goods and ends, the self-certain 'absolute' world of goods, that the material ethics of value could arise. It presumes Kant's destruction of these kinds of ethics."[8] Moreover, his writings after the First World War contain ideas about a growing culture of equalization (*Ausgleichskultur*). He seems to have something like a cosmopolitan ethos in view, which was of course not something that he wanted to ground through philosophical argument; he was trying to predict its necessary rise.

Finally in this connection, it should be mentioned that the concept of the person assumes a position so central in the world of Scheler's thought (though still within the comprehensive perspective of a theistic metaphysics) that he can say, "The philosophical discipline of ethics can never create moral values: it should never replace the individual conscience."

But what role is left, then, for ethics as a philosophical discipline if one acknowledges that it becomes concrete in the moral knowledge of the person? If it is limited to the qualities and preferences "that are recognized everywhere and by all," is there really any need for philosophy as the "scientific presentation of what is thus recognized"? Before, philosophy could claim that it could clarify values, that there exists a completely superior ethical knowledge through "wisdom." But is there any need for philosophy then? For correcting what presumption? The most important, indeed, is the one it has itself created. . . .

Clearer, though making even larger claims, is the way Nicolai Hartmann addresses this issue. Needless to say, he does not at all overlook the fact that the feeling of value is prior to all philosophical research. But the pathos of this research, in which he considered himself something of a pioneer, was mixed with the pathos of freeing the feeling of value itself. Research in value was supposed to free it from the tyrannical limits that restrict it. Indeed, Hartmann was not afraid of ascribing to philosophical research the function of cultivating the sense of value. Blindness to value, passing by what is valuable, was supposed to be cured by phenomenological research! Hartmann tries to counter the difficulties implicit in such claims for philosophical research by ascribing to it a merely maieutic function, not a prescriptive or a descriptive one. This is in itself an ingenious idea, if we think, as we should, about the originator of this metaphor of midwifery, Plato's Socrates. The maieutics of Socrates serves to cure the madness of thinking that everyone always already knows all genuine "virtues," and the Socratic dialectic has a positive function as well. It leads to recognition of what is genuinely meant. To cite the most important example of *anamnesis* in Plato: true courage does not consist in holding one's position in the face of obvious danger, but in being watchful for the greatest, because least observed, danger—seduction by what is pleasant, especially flattery (*Republic* IV).[9] For Plato's Socrates, achieving moral knowledge has the structure of recognition, and it is renewed precisely as a mythic heritage; this is what justifies Socrates' often forceful style of rebuttal. He tries to make it evident that the right thing is what we really meant, and that this should be maintained against all error and confusion. From this point of view both Plato's appropriation of the Pythagorean religion of souls and his acceptance of the Ideas become intelligible. Hartmann's appeal to the maieutics of Socrates therefore seems well grounded.

In the Platonic dialogues, however, it is always knowing that one does not know—as we can always interpret this Socratic irony—that persuades the other that he does not know either, and that transfers the unwavering search for the logos from the questioner to the answerer. It is not the behavior of a researcher, trying to make universally valid scientific statements, but rather a paradigm of moral self-inquiry and self-knowledge, and in any case something that gets built up only dialogically and takes effect only in that way as well. Plato is obviously aware of precisely this: what is at issue here is not something that can be taught (*Epistle* VII, 341c, ῥητὸν γὰρ οὐδαμῶς ἐστιν ὡς ἄλλα μαθήματα).

The *Seventh Letter* merely expresses in the abstract what the Socratic dialogues practice in the concrete. Thus I fall back into my old doubts and ask once again how the task of a philosophical ethics of value squares with the unbreakable imperatives of a lived ethos. Can what is meant by the concept of "value" escape the dilemma of either being relative to a dominant ethos or raising a claim to absoluteness that can be fulfilled only at the remove of research—by "knowing at a distance"? This in general is what I asked myself then (and still do today).[10]

I am of course quite aware that the a priori nature of value that Scheler and Hartmann defended and their talk of "intuiting" values, of laws for choosing among values, of value syntheses, and so on, have since been exposed to a radical critique that was directed against the phenomenological conception of intuition generally and that recognizes language usage alone as the sole ground of all genuine evidence. It is indisputable that "analytic philosophy" has put a decisive stop to the unclear mixing of practical-moral knowledge and theoretical research, much to the benefit of the latter. Just after the Second World War, I recall being informed by the critique of "analytical" ethics in Collingwood's autobiography. Since then, partly under the influence of Wittgenstein, there has been a great stream of attempts to clarify the logic of normative propositions. This, of course, is completely contrary to the notion that value is a priori. Just as the traditional problems of metaphysics were considered exposed as mystifications produced by language, so too the ethics of value collapsed along with its claim to possess its own realm of a priori knowledge, prior to all actual practical insight and decision. Everything that was the subject of research was merely ways of using words—that is, those that carry a normative sense. We can see that such meta-ethical "reflexivity" takes as its object one aspect of moral reality. These are new developments that I do not feel qualified to assess.

Only one thing might be said: it remains an open question, I think, whether the use of words and the structure of sentences in which such usages are found can do justice to the originality implicit in normative experience. For usage includes an element of critique with respect to the conventionality of norms and their verbal expression. The moral consciousness does not content itself with merely applying rules. Scheler was quite right when (in the quotation cited above) he limits the claims of philosophical ethics. Precisely here is to be found the root of our discomfort with grounding moral laws "theoretically" and so too with language analysis.

This is not to deny that evaluating the behavior of others belongs just as much to normative experience as does the self-examination that reaches its high point in the subtle stirrings of conscience. Neither is to be divided from the other. Both are involved in the cultivation of moral standards in the individual and society alike. Thus the distinction of English moral philosophy has always been to have taken up the ancient tradition of Aristotle and considered the various attitudes that emerge in recognition, praise, commendation, consecration, and their opposites. Even phenomenological research in value (Dietrich von Hildebrand) has given consideration to "value-answers" as evidence, and Hartmann gratefully utilized this contribution.[11] To be sure, all of what emerge in Greek ethics as opinions (δοκοῦντα) and assertions of value (λεγόμενα) belong to the givenness of the normative. But beginning with the "Daß" of normative validity (ἀρχὴ γὰρ τὸ ὅτι—by this is meant the λεγόμενα), which lends Aristotle's grounding of practical philosophy a universal validity that is inescapable and indubitable, can (under the presupposition of "practical philosophy") only legitimate the fact that limiting it to the universality of types includes at the same time the return path to the concreteness of normative experience. This emerges clearly in Aristotle's appeal to the seemly (ὡς δεῖ), to the σπουδαῖος, and so on. Aristotle is quite right as well when in the same sense he characterizes the free citizen (whom he always has in mind) as having prohairesis—that is, being able to make the choice of "life," giving preference to one "life" above others. This does not at all undercut the "absolute" validity of arete and the rank ordering of the *bioi* within which given "choices of preference" play themselves out in the concrete. Universalization, then, does not involve distanciation into the theoretical, but belongs essentially to the rationality of moral experience itself. This is the decisive thing, however: all universalization presupposes the normative validity of a ruling ethos and one's being raised in it; it is not something of which one becomes aware in a theoretical manner, but rather by entering into the concrete logos of moral awareness and choice. It is to mistake the obvious when the virtue of reasonableness, of phronesis, is reduced to practicality, *prudentia,* cleverness in life. This is an error that I find again today in K. O. Apel, among others.[12] Kant is not guilty of making it, as demonstrated by his distinction between technical and practical imperatives and his elaboration of the "pure" practical reason, which shows the essential contents of enlightened humanism in practice. But in the period that immediately followed, practical reason was once again aligned with instrumental rationality—an error that dominated the whole critique of Kant's moral philosophy from Hegel to Simmel and Scheler, and that Nicolai Hartmann, as a defender of Kant, opposed at least in principle. Gerhard Krüger[13] then showed how the critique of Kant had totally misunderstood the function of the typic of moral judgment—not to speak of Scheler's short-circuited, ideological misunderstanding of Kant's concept of duty. Duty has nothing of blind slavishness about it; on the contrary, it represents the concretion of practical reason.

Now, the unity of a lived ethos—which gives practical reason its content—is certainly not a given in the age of ethical, ethnic, and historical pluralism; thus the question arises as to how ethical propositions that retain the normative sense of the ethical are at all possible. I have shown above that phenomenological research into a priori values, as well as the research program of moral language analysis, cannot be integrated into the rationality specific to practical reason as such. Kant's successful proof of the categorical validity of the moral law remains in place, in comparison to the conditional nature of all rules of expediency. This is precisely the meaning of "formalism" in ethics. According to Kant, as is well known, the moral law applies to rational beings generally, not just to men, and in truth it establishes not the content of morality, but only the categorical nature of moral obligation. Nevertheless, the question arises of whether in our pluralistic world, too, this universal validity implies something for that solidarity between peoples that we call humanity and that allows Kant to present a differentiated doctrine of duties in his *Metaphysics of Morals*. It remains uncertain whether some future world culture will succeed in overcoming all distances and relativities, unifying the moral concepts and moral systems of humanity in one common ethos, perhaps in view of the ecological crisis or the danger of atomic war that threatens the future of all humanity. But it seems clear that only then will it become possible for practical philosophy to communicate the universal validity of its insights to the normative consciousness and its concretion in the consciousness of each person. This would return practical philosophy to its ancient privilege of not merely recognizing the good, but demanding it as well.

This scarcely means that Greek ethics would be rehabilitated in terms of content—more likely that the methodological ideal of practical philosophy would be reestablished. It would become "ethics" again—that is, it would give a general account not of the contents of a consciousness of value, but of the whole reality lived in law and custom, that is, in ethos (ἔθος and ἦθος). Thereby one element of Greek ethics would receive special significance: the dominant role played by friendship, *philia*. A good quarter of Aristotle's *Ethics* is devoted to the problem of friendship, and the catalogues of almost all the later moral philosophers of Greece list massive books on friendship. When I began my teaching career in 1929, I lectured on "The Role of Friendship in Greek Ethics" and indicated the difference between that and the modern role.[14] Two extensive books of the *Nicomachean Ethics* deal with the subject—whereas Kant's moral philosophy friendship merits only a single page! Starting from modern concepts it is admittedly difficult to define the place of friendship. In certain respects that is true for the conceptual self-understanding of the Greeks as well. It is no arete, no hexis—that is, no ontological quality of a person. It is a good, certainly, and perhaps one of the highest goods of human life. But, as a good, friendship far surpasses the realm of moral responsibility for oneself—like all "goods." It is a good bestowed on us, not a "value" of which we are conscious. Friendship is no personal quality. One must be capable of friendship, of course (and that involves all kinds of personal qualities, the gift for sympathy, self-criticism, and a capacity for making contact), but equally belonging to friendship are connections and a favorable moment to make them, and above all—good fortune. No more than love can friendship be summoned on demand.

For these reasons, friendship reaches far beyond the pleasure experienced when an individual who gives himself to the other in *eros* and philia rises above the narrow sphere of self-concern; it points to that ultimate dimension of things that we share, on which social life as a whole depends and without which no institutional system of communal life—whether constitution, legal system, or bureaucracy—is able to fulfill its function. An old maxim of the Greek ethics of friendship says it all: "among friends everything is common" (κοινὰ τὰ τῶν φίλων). Ultimately it means not only the world of goods, of possessions and enjoyments, and not just reciprocal sympathy and inclination; it includes the solidarity that exercises a dominion extending far beyond everything conscious, everything desired, into trade and business, political life, and work life, as well as into the intimacy of family and home. It stretches out over the whole realm that the Greeks called "praxis," and this is what distinguishes the idea of practical philosophy. Not just that "theoria" is itself a kind of praxis, as Aristotle well knew. Where "praxis" becomes the object of "theoria," and such is the case in "practical philosophy," the "method" of conceptual analysis is grounded upon the commonalities that bind us all—these represent the real thing for which we are one and all called to account as human beings: our own practical reasonableness.

8

Reflections on the Relation of Religion and Science (1984)

In our time religion finds itself in a unique situation. For the first time the important thing is no longer the *pro* and *contra* that have been connected from time immemorial with the claim that religions raise. It is no longer waging war for the true god against the false ones or defending one's own religion against the attacks of unbelievers, whether those belonging to another faith or that of scientific atheism. Today the issue is much more the question whether humanity needs religion at all. Of course, the critique of religion in the manner of Epicurus, Feuerbach, and Marx, as well as of Freud, long ago posed this question and anticipated the answer. But the uniqueness of today's situation seems to me that even the question about the meaning of religion becomes pointless when more and more people actually live without religion. The atheism of indifference does not even recognize the question anymore. Has the end of an illusion arrived? Or is precisely that the illusion: thinking that human beings can live without religion?

The question has changed in the process of scientific and technological civilization being spread over the whole earth. What, exactly, are we asking about when we think of religion? Christendom's apologia, as found in Pascal or Dostoyevski, has in mind the Christian faith and its response to the special challenge presented by the anti-theology of the modern Enlightenment. Fundamentally this was a conflict among faiths. The Enlightenment movement ushered in by science obviously had an ideological element of its own.

Now it might be thought that modernity's faith in science had in fact gone far beyond defining itself by opposition to the Christian church, and had thereby amalgamated the concept of religion in a certain unity as a counterconcept to the Enlightenment. From the standpoint of modern science this is logical; thus Max Weber drew this conclusion in his well-known thesis concerning the demystification of the world. Clearly, however, the situation is far more complex. Observers of the contemporary world can adduce a great deal of evidence for the continued life of religious energies and renewed religious impulses even in the age of science.

In itself this is hardly surprising when we recall the convincing way Kant compared the idea of modern science and the ancient tradition of metaphysics. His *Critique of Pure Reason* indeed represents critical limitations on the truth claim of science. To what extent does modern faith in science affect all our thinking about the nature and future of religion? It is apparent that the concept of demystification, which in fact implies its opposite, is conceived from the viewpoint of rationally mastering the world. Even Max Weber's conception of scientific enlightenment and the irreversible processes rationalizing social life is cognizant of limits, however. Thus Max Weber discusses charismatics and himself recognizes that there are situations where the choices exceed any possibility of making rational decisions, and where each one of us must follow his god. Now, this is obviously not conceptualized on the basis of scientific rationality. Today what is a matter of discussion is not so much the limits of science, which Max Weber did not overlook, but the question of whether appropriate access to religion can ever be found by beginning with the modern Enlightenment's concept of knowledge.

The shadows thrown by the scientific approach to the world truly reach beyond all limits. Insofar as science views everything that can be experienced as its possible object, it must from that point of view consign everything "beyond" to the subjective side. Precisely in doing so it must make these subjective modes of comportment once again into objects. Now, representing the merely subjective is the generic concept of feeling, and this concept is of such indeterminate contours that it completely dissolves in the world of what is experienced as fact. One might think of the whole realm of emotional thought, of Carnap's well-known polemic against Heidegger's discourse about nothing, as well as of the critique of Schleiermacher's theology of feeling.

The concept of faith, however, is uniquely suspended between a truth claim that lags behind knowing and a certainty that knowing lags behind ("Do not doubt of what you cannot see"). This is a highly questionable place for the concept of faith. To be sure, modern Cartesian science was not the first to articulate the religious meaning of this concept. The relation of *credo* and *intelligo*, *pistis* and *gnosis*, is inherent in the Judeo-Christian tradition. This indeed is what accounts for the fact that modern science-based culture is both definitive and problematical, that it comprehends the whole earth, yet is formed by Christendom, where the Judaic emphasis on personality and Greek rationality are united. Modern civilization based on science has achieved such technological superiority in controlling the powers of nature that no other culture can displace it, even if it is rooted in a completely different religious tradition.

What does this mean for us today? The concept of faith can scarcely claim to apply to the whole planet in the same way as the concept of science. Even in our very own European tradition there are problems to be found. The question of faith is entirely avoided by the life forms of Greek religion. Obeying the cult's laws and honoring the gods can even accord with atheistic doctrines, as shown by the surprising phenomenon of

Lucretius's didactic poem; and even in the Roman Catholic Church not only is it the case that true faith is defined entirely by the authority of the church, but what is finally decisive is participation in the church as a medium of grace. Cultic practice is accorded all the subjective certainty that can be called the certainty of faith. Reformation Christianity was the first to impel the original Christian gospel into the extremes of faith and doubt in such a way that the individual was forced to make the wager of faith (as of doubt)—like the "true" and "false" in knowledge. But whereas science offers theoretical knowledge by which the individual understands himself to be supported and thus unburdened, in making the wager of faith, the Protestant is left all to himself—that is, to the evidence of God's grace that lights his way. The concept of revelation is of course connected to the church, the communion of saints, even in Protestant Christendom. But even the church service—proclaiming the healing power of God-become-man and redemption through Jesus—is grounded on the preacher's testimony of faith.

This is a very slender basis for understanding religion. Such a reduction of religion to the certainty of faith is clearly in accord with the subjectivist thinking of modernity. It seems evident that, in following the principle of self-consciousness, one takes up a viewpoint that claims truly universal breadth and that therefore comprehends all other possible kinds of human behavior, including even comportment toward the holy. But it is just as evident that the primacy of self-consciousness is no longer uncontested; it has been shaken to its very foundation by ideology critique, by Nietzsche, and by Freud. This is not to say, of course, that the critique of religion and of Christianity have really left behind the principle of self-consciousness. There is always behind it the true consciousness of an emancipated humanity, the reacquired innocence of becoming, or a human nature that has become wholly transparent to itself. But it is precisely here that the question arises whether the methodological premises upon which modern science is grounded, the ideal of method and objectivization, do not necessarily misrepresent the phenomena with which we are here concerned. On this path the science of religion comes to be the science of how consciousness is susceptible to illusion, and this means that it can and should become the science of what people in various religions, cultures, and times have "believed."

This often leads to embarrassments, of course. Thus, in the tradition of Greek religious thought we find remarkable juxtapositions—for example, between the behavior of the gods to men and conscious human behavior. This is something that Lesky, in connection with B. Snell, has previously showed in Homer. Or in the realm of Christian theology we find a mythological or an existential understanding of the promise of the gospel and, sharpened to the ultimate degree, human self-understanding in both worldly and transcendent terms. The Enlightenment schema of the demystification of the world, the irreversible path from mythos to logos, seems too simple.

Let us consider for a moment the contrary thesis: that the modern scientific enlightenment presents only a partial view of the world, one that occurs only to someone with a universal faith in science and that is therefore ideologically suspect. Evidence of this is that virtually everything opposed to such one-sidedness is driven out, as if by misdirected religious energies. In any case, the concept of religion and religious behavior assumes a new ambiguity. From the standpoint of the enlighteners, religion reflects merely the childhood of humanity. Yet everywhere are manifest the powers that in the most various ways legitimate a view of the matter opposed to that of science. For example, there is the appeal to the continued life of religious creeds in the social movements of our time. I refer not only to the unbroken traditions of the great religious communities, such as the Roman Catholic and Greek Orthodox churches, but also to the almost inconceivable stability of Islam, which affirms the unity of political, legal, and literal religious truths, and therefore limits the influence of modern science-based culture. Beyond this, there are the completely impenetrable traditions of Asia, on which the scientific and technical thought of the West is simply superimposed, and in our own Christian church we see revival movements of the most various kinds. The question often arises as to what extent it is really religious motives that impel such movements, or whether this receptiveness to solidarity is actually being exploited for the purpose of other kinds of solidarity, to nationalistic, racist, political, or economic ends. But even if so, such exploitation would indicate something. The possibility must always be considered that the social function thus performed does not entirely discredit its religious background. It has always been the case that religious movements are connected with social impulses.

But we must make room for another consideration as well: to what extent should ersatz religions be kept in mind—for instance, the solidarity of sports fans or the fanaticism of political demonstrations—or even the artificial practice of political world views—for example, in the form of the Führer cult or under the banner of class conflict whose extra-religious purposes are obvious. Must we not admit that such movements can lead to solidarities that project an image—and perhaps not just an image—which is completely consistent with that of traditional religious practices? If it is said that they are created and not real, on what is this judgment based? The immense experience that this century has had with so-called brainwashing, not necessarily that effected by drugs or torture, warns us to be careful.

Finally, we need to recognize the genuine forms of religious solidarity that stem from insight into the breakup of religious traditions: for example, moral or political solidarities or those built upon mystical pantheism or altruistic *caritas*. Such intellectual movements are sometimes incapable of being institutionalized and are sometimes as short-lived as the subcultural sects; yet the significance of these intellectual movements in the social life of our times ought not be underestimated. Thanks to the mass media, they have an enormous coefficient for multiplication. The susceptibility of public consciousness to being affected from without has risen immeasurably. Ultimately we must ask to what extent pure empirical research is really capable of understanding religious phenomena as such, or whether such phenomena are not always to be observed only through their social effects. If so, the question arises as to what, exactly, "genuine" means.

In particular, we might ask whether common convictions are not capable of reformulating themselves in numerous novel ways, not at all dissolving into the alternative world history proffered by centralized totalitarianism or economic liberalism. Are there not experiences of being overwhelmed? Today we have the problems of ecology, the economics of energy, and world hunger that certainly do not stop at political borders, and where the conflict of interests becomes more and more important. Even when these do not eventuate in dramatic crises, our experience of the industrial age teaches us that all possibilities are limited, and that limiting and circumscribing ourselves is therefore necessary. In the final analysis humanity is faced with imminent disillusionment concerning the power of human beings over nature and perhaps, even more, concerning the control of human suffering. In this way, thought is evidently directed back to the fundamental question to which religions have always offered their answers. Thus the question arises as to whether we are ultimately using concepts that are at all appropriate when we approach religions from the point of view of scientific knowledge and inquire about the extent to which their certainties derive from a "genuine" faith that must forever remain scientifically unprovable.

It is this doubt that invites us to go back behind the conceptual opposition between faith and knowledge to the old opposition between mythos and logos. Mythos and logos seem more compatible with each other; indeed, they seem precisely complementary. The concept of mythos originating in antiquity is undisseverably tied to the ancient concept of the divine. The mythos tells a story of the divine. But it tells only a story. There are stories of gods and stories of gods and men that point to the dimension of the divine. It is obvious, and probably not limited to Greek antiquity, that in such stories what is told is not the object of one's own knowledge, a belief or faith held to be indubitable. Rather, stories are much more like living memorials erected in immediate memory of dynasties, tribes and towns, locales and landscapes. The transition from stories to the mythic is fluid, and the stories themselves are fluid, in that they are continually refurbished by virtually limitless poetic invention, just as by the genial tellers of fairy tales that we are familiar with. But this is clear: the story is about gods known as the world.

Of course, the relation of mythos to logos is not entirely without tension.[1] A myth is always only believable, not "true." But the kind of credibility that a myth has is not just *Wahrscheinlichkeit* (verisimilitude, probability, true-seemingness) deficient in demonstrated certainty; it bears its own riches within it, the *Schein des Wahren* (radiance, bank note, appearance of the true), the sameness of semblance in which the true appears. This truth is, to be sure, not the story itself, for it can be told in various ways; it is what appears in it—not just something that is meant, something that would always need to be verified, but what becomes present in it.

Here, moreover, aspects of Christian culture find a new significance. In this connection I think in particular of the narrative form of thought and the ritual form of language that have long occupied me as philosophical problems.[2]

In any case, taking account of this dimension of the mythic is a philosophical task of its own—at least for the European tradition of philosophy that lives with an eye on science. In this connection we recall the word used by Schelling, "das Unvordenkliche" (what cannot be thought in advance). In this we see our own problem as bringing the objectivizing tendency of consciousness (not just that of modern science) into balance with mythic experience. Schelling's word gives resounding expression to what we are looking for when we speak of mythic experience. But the word *unvordenklich* articulates something unreachable by the longing of thought and, from that viewpoint, something that is therefore not described in terms of its own being and appearance. Most fundamentally, what seems to me to point in the right direction is still Heidegger's concept of "Andenken," which has its origin in Hegel's philosophy of religion and designates the connection between health and the holy. This is indicative of the experience with which we are concerned here. Just as health is not known in the same way as a wound or disease, so the holy is perhaps more a way of being than of being believed.

9

Friendship and Self-Knowledge: Reflections on the Role of Friendship in Greek Ethics (1985)

When I began teaching at the university in 1928 and chose "The Role of Friendship in Philosophical Ethics" as the topic of my inaugural lecture at Marburg, I was primarily motivated by two impulses. One was Heidegger's warning, often since repeated, "We still do not think of the Greeks in a way that is Greek enough." I became particularly aware of this when, coming from Kant's ethics of duty and phenomenological ethics of value, I was confronted with Aristotle's ethics. This was what determined the course of thought in my inaugural lecture. There was, however, another motive, of a distant origin, in operation here: the neo-Kantian critique of transcendental Idealism emerging after the First World War. It began with the early work of Friedrich Gogarten, Martin Buber (and behind him Franz Rosenzweig), Ferdinand Ebner, and Theodor Haecker, and it found its most influential embodiment in Karl Barth's commentary on the Epistle to the Romans. There is to be found the insight that the concepts of contemporary transcendental philosophy do not suffice to comprehend what makes the discourse of God possible.

Basically we all needed to get a sense for the first time of what it was we were looking for. After the liberal period's optimism about progress was shattered following the catastrophe of the First World War, we needed to construct a new understanding of human (and also civic) community. The consciousness of a deep crisis pertained just as much to the human relation to God as to the "worldly" relation of "community and society." Until then, still most influential were the conceptual presuppositions of neo-Kantianism (in particular the key concept of "consciousness as such") and the grounding of modern thought on the certainty of self-consciousness—despite Nietzsche and his followers. This influence was evident even as late as Husserl's turn toward "transcendental phenomenology." In the nonconcept of "intersubjectivity" that occupied Husserl's tireless efforts to ground the move to the "other" upon his Cartesian and neo-Kantian heritage, this became ever clearer. Then came Heidegger. He showed that "subjectivity" retained a Greek conceptual schema that only an ontology of the present at hand could satisfy. He made it evident what it means that both "subiectum" and "substantia" point back to the ὑποκείμενον: the "enduring" substance that remains despite the mutability of accidents and that refers to the τί of "essentia." The understanding of being defined in the Greek way did not square with the self-understanding of humanity formed by Christianity. And it did not measure up to the problem of historical relativism at all. Thus Heidegger's own beginning point, the discovery of the temporal character of "existence," was truly epoch-making. This necessarily directed my attention to the fact that a phenomenon like friendship, its consistency and constancy, could not be properly understood by beginning with self-consciousness.

I was impelled in the same direction, however, by the philological research of the time, especially that of Karl Reinhardt and Paul Friedländer, who were working on Nietzsche and George ("The circle closed by love"). Moreover, Bruno Snell's bold critique of applying Aristotle's concept of προαίρεσις to early Greek poetry,[1] a practice rampant in the school of Werner Jaeger, offered a good deal to think about. The "action of drama" undeniably points to another dimension of experience than that of purpose and will. Applying Aristotle's doctrine of προαίρεσις to the earlier periods of Greek poetry was misleading.[2] Later, Hermann Langerbeck's long-undervalued study[3] pointed me in a similar direction. It opened my eyes to anachronisms commonly found in interpretations of the Presocratics and their concepts—for example, when νοεῖν is translated as "thought."

From that point on, it became unintelligible that for a century "Homeric theology" had been considered a mere sideline to Christian theology and that no one had viewed it, rather, as a poetic reordering concealing a many-faceted religious tradition ruled by completely different abysses and obscurities than the gods playing upon sunny Olympus would lead one to suspect. We took inspiration from Nietzsche's philosophical transport, as we began to realize that with Homer a significant step had been taken toward the brightness of thought. Conversely, on the other side, the Socratic turn and the way it was worked out by Plato had to be abstracted from false modernization, from Kant as from modern philosophy as a whole, even from the late Hellenistic appropriation of εἰς ἑαυτόν. From the impossible, neoscholastic translation of φιλία as "love among friends" (*Freundschaftsliebe*), for example, it appeared that a genuine encounter of thought with the Greeks was obstructed by false assimilations. Thus we needed to ask what function the Socratic-Platonic turn to "inward beauty" actually performed. Might an extended discussion of the problem of friendship in Greek philosophy offer an answer?

Upon rereading my unpublished lecture notes after fifty-five years, it appears to me that this was what led me to pursue the subject at that time. Today I would like to try once again to take up the problem already discerned in the three treatments of friendship and clarify it further. Here I can rely on the philological research represented by Dirlmeier, Gigon, and Fraisse,[4] among others, without availing myself of such other materials as philosophical phenomenology, just as I did in the case of my 1928 inaugural lecture. Working out the structure of friendship shows that, by its very nature, friendship cannot be the business of the one or the other. So much is obvious; but it is just this which for Aristotle constitutes both ethics and politics together as practical philosophy. This was the first thing that needed to be worked out in opposition to the modern philosophy dominated by the primacy of self-consciousness. The embarrassment in which the philosophical foundations of the modern social sciences find themselves consists in the fact that the ontological constitution of society cannot be at all properly understood from the modern nominalist viewpoint that gave birth to modern science. In this regard, modern subjectivist thought must be forced to concede that "mind" must also, and preeminently, be thought of as objective mind, for as such it forms state and society. Hegel understood this and, by implication, everything else that has since occurred in the sciences of state and society. But what did the Greeks, who had no such concept of science and of "mind," think about this? The fact that Plato could think of world, city, and soul all in one, and that Aristotle, despite detaching ethics from the universal teleology of the good, avoided narrowing it to an ethics of disposition, and placed φιλία alongside ἀρετή, makes Greek practical philosophy in many respects a paradigm for the critique of subjectivity that still occupies our thought today.

Thus in the 1928 presentation I pursued the structure of self-relatedness that cannot be reduced to the structure of subjectivity, but rather is played out beyond it.[5] This is what the doctrine of friendship has to teach, in particular the role that self-love and self-sufficiency play in it. I had already recognized this in 1928, but that part of my lecture no longer strikes me as sufficient, so I will try to improve it. At issue are three questions:

1. What do the kinds of friendship mean for the nature of friendship?
2. What can it mean to say that φιλαυτία, self-love, is the basis of friendship?[6]
3. Why must autarchy or self-sufficiency be superseded for the sake of friendship?[7]

For all three questions the background is obviously Plato, especially the *Lysis,* but also the *Republic.* We need to take into consideration all three treatises of Aristotle—the *Nicomachean Ethics,* the *Eudemian Ethics,* and the *Magna Moralia.* These texts offer little indication of their development. All three are related to Plato, and all three illustrate Aristotle's tendency not to envision practical philosophy on the basis of metaphysics or theology, but rather to erect it on the concrete basis of moral and political experience and its expression in ruling ideas. Today I consider it no longer practicable to force it into the schema of a history of development.

All three treatises introduce a distinction between three kinds of friendship, a doctrine that retained its validity until the eighteenth century. Utility, pleasantness, and excellence (χρήσιμον, ἡδύ, κατ' ἀρετήν) are the three elements that distinguish various kinds of friendship as φιλητόν. These three kinds are not in the strict sense kinds of friendship within a common genus. Aristotle makes that clear. Rather, friendship grounded in ἀρετή takes absolute precedence. In the *Eudemian Ethics* it is explicitly called the "First" (*H* 2, 1236b3 f.)—obviously appealing to Plato's discussion of the πρῶτον φίλον in the *Lysis* (220d). The other forms of friendship are related to this first one, which most fully fulfills the idea of friendship. Thus the *Nicomachean Ethics* too calls it "complete" (τελεία: Θ

5, 1156b34). Clearly what is being discussed is not the διαίρεσις of a γένος in its εἴδη, but rather an analogical relation to a First—as, for example, the being of the categories is related to the being of substance (*Cat.* 5, 2a11 and 2b8). The *Eudemian Ethics* illustrates the kinds of friendship by means of the same comparison as Aristotle uses for the problem of the categories (*H* 2 1236a16 ff.) when he says, "It is not just the person that is healthy, the color of a face is healthy, and also food and such." The *Metaphysics* too draws an analogy with the concept of healthfulness (Γ: 2, 1003b1 ff.), but in a different way than in the *Ethics*. Here it is described with another variation: "healthy is the soul, healthy is the body, healthy is the medicine," and so on. This illustration of the multivocity of "healthy" or "health-ful" (ἰατρικός) should, in the case of kinds of friendship, be taken as applying to the difference between ψυχή and σῶμα. We need to pay special attention to this. The dependence of the body on the soul and the soul on the body is clearly not the same kind of thing, so that one could simply draw a distinction as between two kinds of health. Not only is the soul nothing but the entelechy of the body, as Aristotle teaches, but the healthfulness of the body too is indivisible from the psychosomatic nexus, and this is something ancient medicine was well aware of.

Furthermore, the distinction between "kinds" of friendship is not strict or exact, so true friendship always exists within all limited kinds of friendship. What is under discussion, therefore, is not, as with substance and accidents, the *prius* in the expression and its ontological corollary, the substance, but rather the perfection, the true essence, which in other kinds of friendship is only *partly* realized, yet realized in such a way that it is still meaningful to inquire into what they have in common. Perfect friendship, then, is not a genus. Like modifications, the other forms of friendship depend on the full meaning of friendship.

Aristotle shows, however, that they have the same conceptual structure. First of all, it is reciprocal (ἀντιφίλησις). This is completely realized in the friendship grounded in ἀρετή. But there is also something of it in love or business relationships. In all three kinds, something more must be added to reciprocity: namely, that in their being good to one another the partners cannot remain concealed from each other. Finally, the other forms of friendship can approximate full friendship more and more closely. The bond of love can be of such a kind that over the long term it turns into the bond of genuine friendship, and the same is true of business friends who form a lasting friendship, sometimes even for generations. Distinct from these are other relationships that are admittedly similar, yet are not "friendship." Thus it is clear that merely being well disposed to someone (as in προαίρεσις) or having good will toward someone is not friendship. Even if this sympathy or good will were actually to occur on both sides and to that extent constitute reciprocity, it would be mere friendliness so long as the two people were not really openly bound to each other. The *common* condition of all "friendship" is more than that: the true bond that—in various degrees—signifies a "life together" (συζῆν). This Aristotle knew.

Now, in the analysis of true—that is, perfect—friendship there is one point in particular that represents Aristotle's heritage from Plato to an unusual degree: φιλαυτία, or self-love, which we can say first makes full φιλία possible. As friendship with oneself, it leads Aristotle's analyses in the *Nicomachean Ethics,* as well as in the other treatises, to their highest point. This is paradoxical in a certain sense. It is certainly enlightening that reciprocal love, manifest as such, occurs in friendship, so that we can speak of two partners at all. But is this possible with reference to oneself? Are the parts of the soul really like separate partners—even though Plato introduces them thus in the *Republic?* Is not Aristotle right when (in the books on the soul) he lets the parts of the soul retreat into the background[8] in view of the unity of the living being, and when in the *Ethics* he distinguishes them in a merely analytical and expository way? In truth he separates ethical and dianoetic ἀρετή, ὄρεξις, and νοῦς only in order to consider them indivisible in the unity of human nature.

Given Plato's fundamental distinction between two parts of the soul, one rational and one "alogical" or emotional, it is of course natural to begin with a duality. The unification and unity of the two "soul parts" in friendship may then be like "one soul," as two inseparable friends are called. The *Nicomachean Ethics* actually describes what Aristotle calls friendship with oneself in such a way that the unity of the soul is, so to speak, fully realized in it; and there he discerns the structure of all true friendship.[9] Only among the "good" or in the σπουδαῖος can there be such a friendship with oneself. Clearly there can be no such thing among animals. Because they know no conflict between instinct and reason (*Eudemian Ethics H* 6, 1240b32), they can neither lack nor possess unity and oneness with themselves.

Aristotle is quite aware of the paradox in Plato's doctrine: namely, that someone must be friends with himself in order to befriend someone else. This hardly answers to the usual preconception of friendship and self-love. Thus Aristotle considers himself specially obliged to discuss the aporias of self-love. Clearly he defends its Platonic meaning as opposed to that of common usage. We first find the word φιλαυτία in Aristotle, admittedly; but as a moral problem this subject is well known and quite certainly much older, at least in the form that one's being dominated by self-love makes one incapable of friendship. The illusions of self-love, like following one's own interests egoistically, belong to human nature generally. This is also confirmed by the fact that Aristotle's texts presume that the word φιλαυτία is to be used in a critical, pejorative sense. Evidence of this is not far to seek. I mean, tragedy, like comedy, continually forces us to see its consequences—being tragically or comically blinded—and Plato expressly warns us in the *Laws* (V, 731d ff.) about the σφόδρα ἑαυτοῦ φιλία. The question should be put the other way: whether a positive sense of self-love did not emerge for the first time in the age of Socrates. Perhaps in the Sophists, in Protagoras or Democritus, or wherever the pathways of natural-law thinking were under consideration? Perhaps in the Socratics themselves, when they sacrificed all to the ascetic self-sufficiency of the wise—or in a man like Eudoxos who integrated human life with the life of all other beings in the sense that all are driven by the same demand for ἡδονή? Did Eudoxos thus describe the ὄρεξις ἑαυτοῦ, for example? Be that as it may, it is not without hesitation that Aristotle employs "intercourse with oneself" and "friendship with oneself" as possible locutions and takes them as prefigurations of complete friendship.[10]

Apparently, for Aristotle full friendship with oneself came too close to the ideal of autarchy. He knew how closely autarchy is tied to eudaimonia, but he knew as well that when someone is wholly sufficient unto himself, something essential is missing from true perfection. What is lacking is precisely the increase that friendship signifies. If self-love is to have a positive sense, it can nevertheless not go so far in that direction that someone thinks he needs no friends. In all three of Aristotle's treatments, therefore, the discussion of autarchy is carried on in connection with self-love. Aristotle does not go to the extreme of such full autarchy as occurs, for example, in the Stoic ideal of wisdom. Rather, it seems to me that he expressly oversteps the ideal of complete self-possession precisely because he wants to draw a line dividing him from those Socratics who have taken Socrates' admonition about concern for oneself to a cynical extreme.

His main argument sounds strange enough, given modern habits of thought, and it comes out far too unmediated. He says that the essence of a friend consists in someone's being able to understand his neighbor more easily than himself. To understand this argument, we need to consider how strong in everyone is the pressure toward illusions about themselves. That is clearly what Aristotle has in mind. We blame others for what really pertains to ourselves. The New Testament says it in this way: we see the mote in the eye of another and not the beam that is in our own. In this sense self-knowledge is in fact a difficult task, never completely to be accomplished.

In the *Magna Moralia* Aristotle explicitly alludes to the fact that self-knowledge is required of the wise (B 15, 1213a13 ff.). There he might be thinking of Socrates and his admonition, and he certainly is referring to the older moral gnomicism. In any case, it belongs to the deepest consciousness of a human being that he needs to know about himself, that he is no god. Reminding us of this was the point of the Delphic oracle's imperative. When Aristotle appeals to it here, he intends it merely in the practical sense that someone who follows this admonition will be open to intercourse with others and to the "good."

Yet it seems to me that Aristotle gestures toward the genuine heart of his theory of friendship by comparing it with the divine. Our view of god has two sides. On the one side, we see him as representing perfect existence, and by comparison each of us becomes conscious of our own limitations. From this cognizance of one's own limitations, however, immediately follows that the other, the friend, signifies an accession of being, self-feeling, and the richness of life. Aristotle interprets this to mean that the god who is complete in himself has no friends.[11] This is in fact Aristotelian theology and has application in Aristotelian ethics as well. One must discern the common in the different. The ἐνέργεια, consisting of εὐδαιμονία and φιλία, is not really activity in the sense of depending on an ἔργον, but rather of realizing its own vitality.[12] 'Ενέργεια can always involve both: devotion to others or another and devotion to the realization itself. But even then the essence of the realization of life is still being at one with another, whether the otherness of things or other people. This is true of seeing and perceiving, thinking and knowing. In this self-realization of life, moreover, one's own self is discerned and felt along with the other thing. It is this with-structure that is given with all openness to the world. In being given over to what is discerned, a relation back to the discerner is always in play. This is what is distinctive to us (*Eudemian Ethics H* 12, 1245b16 ff.). But here Aristotle adds: this is, of course, not the way it is for god, since he is superior to the need for uniting with something beyond himself. The ontological level of god is above participating in our well-being. For him, well-being is completely his own, whereas for us it is allotted through another.

This conception of the divine is familiar to us from the onto-theological book Λ (7 ff.) of Aristotle's *Metaphysics*. There, to be sure, the difference between god and man emerges with the opposite intention of making the eminent being of god conceivable by analogy to the finite being of humans. In the *Ethics*, on the other hand, in the process of analyzing human eudaimonia, this difference is turned completely to the advantage of humankind. Via another, a person becomes one with himself. The other, the friend, means much to the person, not because of the person's need or lack, but for the sake of his own self-fulfillment (ἀρετή). The other is like the mirror of self-knowledge. One recognizes himself in another, whether in the sense of taking him as a model, or — and this is even more essential — in the sense of the reciprocity in play between friends, such that each sees a model in the other — that is, they understand one another by reference to what they have in common and so succeed in reciprocal co-perception. Friendship leads to an increase in one's own feeling of life and to a confirmation of one's own self-understanding, as implied in the concept of ἀρετή.

The metaphor of the mirror is already familiar from Plato.[13] Self-knowledge does not mean an interest in oneself as opposed to the other; it pertains precisely to what is common to the one and the other: κατὰ τὸ καλόν. What one sees, with approval or censure, in such a mirror is not the particularity of one's own being but what is binding for oneself as well as for the other, and what one recognizes in the mirror is what otherwise cannot be seen clearly, because of one's weakness. Here the image of the mirror has an indirect power of expression. Seeing oneself in the mirror traverses the entire spectrum, from encounters with what is alien to the fatal self-mirroring of narcissism. In each of these lies a normative element. But encounters in the mirror of the friend are, as always, not experienced as a demand, but rather as a fulfillment. What one encounters there is encountered not as a duty or a command; it is a living counterpart (*ein leibhaftes Gegenüber*). Because this other, this counterpart, is not one's own mirror image, but rather the *friend,* all powers come into play of increasing trust and devotion to the "better self" that the other is for oneself, and that is something more than good resolutions and inward stirrings of conscience. All of it flows into the full stream of self-forming commonalities in which one begins to feel and recognize oneself. What is thus communicated is not just sentiment or disposition; it signifies a real embedding in the texture of communal human life.

This has fundamental anthropological significance. The wisdom of Aristotle recognizes in all human cognition—as in the συμπάθεια—an element of the "with": perceiving-with, knowing-with, thinking-with—that is, living with and being with (*Mitsein*). And Aristotle in no way makes this into a process of reflection where the self or the knowing becomes the object of a reflection. Even when he speaks of κοινὴ αἴσθησις in his theory of perception, this is not a special faculty. Rather, Aristotle is just designating in this manner the dimension of *Mitsein* with oneself that belongs to all perception and thought, and that in the form of φιλία expands to Mitsein with the other.

This is confirmed by the significance of "living with" (συζῆν) for friendship, as well as in the way in which Aristotle counts friends' belonging to each other as true eudaimonia and in his manner of accounting for that. As he understands "self-sufficiency," it is inconceivable without the friends who belong to it. What someone does through a friend, Aristotle says on this point, he does himself. But this is still not the whole story. The true nature of humanity consists in the comparison to the divine. Even this comparison to divine being enters into play here in order to ground the fact that friends are essential in human self-understanding. Through exchange with our friends, who share our views and intentions but who can also correct or strengthen them, we draw nearer to the divine, which possesses continually what is possible for us humans only intermittently: presence, wakefulness, self-presence in "Geist." As natural beings, we humans are divided from ourselves by sleep, just as we are divided from ourselves as intellective beings by forgetting. Yet our friend can keep watch in our place and think for us.

Thus we look out from Aristotle's theory of friendship directly upon his philosophical theology, developed from the Socratic and Platonic question about true being. Complete self-possession is certainly no part of being human. But with Aristotle, as with Euripides, we understand what it means to say: "to know a friend—that too is god."

One final remark might be added that pertains to the significance of both Plato and Aristotle for Christian theology. Plato has certainly spoken not only of a language of searching concepts and the dialectical give and take that underlie the tradition of Greek metaphysics. He spoke as well of a different language that we do not find in Aristotle and that is developed more by the Christian religion and church doctrine than by Aristotle's metaphysics. Plato knew how to combine the language of searching concepts with the language of a people's mythic tradition. Next to the logos strides his use of mythos. On the verbal level of concepts, it seems to me, he consciously draws a halt at the point of thinking of the θεῖον. This is the concept of the divine as unity that everywhere gleams through the great Greek myths as the unity of the divine. Along with this, however, Plato can speak of the gods as something living on through cults and tales in the memory of all. Just as the person following Socrates' admonition concerns himself with and cares for his own soul, so too the gods will succor him with their care and their gifts. That too is Platonic language mixing Plato's own mythic fables with his dialectical concepts.

To be sure, Plato did not take the step that Aristotle did toward a philosophical theology conceptualizing the divine as the one or highest god, the living being who moves all. To that extent Christian theology was right in orienting itself via Aristotle's metaphysics. But the classical Greek theory of friendship has deeper implications. By reason of its Platonic motifs, it could be taken up in the Christian doctrine of love, whose voice resounds even in the modern world dominated by social utilitarianism. Responding to its appeal are forms of life such as marriage and family, solidarity among friends, among people of all ranks and situations, and among all nations and states.

Aristotle and Imperative Ethics (1989)

One essential viewpoint from which to consider human experience of the moral is clearly its imperative character. The practical virtue of phronesis might be rendered as "Sagezza," reasonableness, circumspection, or discretion (*prudentia*). As these equivalents clearly show, "phronesis" can appear to be a merely pragmatic variant, where the strictly binding character of the moral law is watered down into the loose advisability of a discretionary rule. Thus, in his famous grounding of the moral law and its binding nature, Kant contrasted the higher, "categorical" imperative with the imperatives of discretion and cleverness. These relations can be otherwise accented, however. Those like me who took their first philosophical steps in the tradition of neo-Kantianism, and who learned to look with critical eyes by following the controversial figure of Kantian formalism, necessarily missed the richness and breadth of moral truth and reality that is to be found in Aristotle. The rational element in moral behavior, as Aristotle works it out, stands beside ethos in its whole highly differentiated multifariousness. What the Greeks call φρόνησις is an aspect of the essence of moral being that belongs intrinsically to everything that we call "virtue." Ever since Socrates showed that goodness and virtue are not of themselves intelligible and do not consist in selecting and imitating heroic models, the question of the good has been raised to a new level of awareness; it has become mandatory to justify one's own being and behavior and be prepared to explain it. It must be admitted, however, that every attempt to answer Socrates' question about the good always implies an inner connection between ethos and logos, and thus too an equivalence between the adult's becoming socialized through education and training and the logos of justification (*Rechenschaftsgabe*). The name "ethics," introduced by Aristotle, founder of this philosophical discipline, should prevent us from forgetting that, like Plato, Aristotle himself stood in the shadow of the Socratic question. He accepted Socrates' equation of virtue and knowledge in the sense that he incorporated explanation into the moral being of ethos. Thus he founded the tradition that has lived on in our own time as "ethics" or "practical philosophy." It includes not just individuals' attitudes and their system of social life, but the system of social institutions that rule human beings' common life in the social structure. Practical philosophy therefore comprehends not just ethics but also so-called politics, and it refers to both when it is called "practical philosophy."

Now, it says something that the term "politics," title of the second part of Aristotle's practical philosophy, changed in meaning during the course of the nineteenth century. Before then, Aristotle's lecture on politics could and had to be taken as applying to practical philosophy's more general question about the just life. Up to the middle of the nineteenth century, authors writing in German (and presumably those in other languages as well) still understood "politics" as referring to this area of philosophical science. In it was mirrored the claim of philosophy, both familiar and incontestable, to codetermine practice, even that of politics. However, the change in the meaning of "politics" that I have sketched allowed a background of another kind to be seen. Like ethics, politics is constructed upon a presupposition. Ethics—that is, ἠθική, or what is called τὰ ἠθικά in Aristotle's usage—presupposes ethos or mores. Politics presupposes the polis and everything that is implied in this givenness—primarily that a polis has its gods.

Later, this developed in a fundamentally different way, since the Roman Empire took over the sacred functions of Greek-Roman life. Even the "civitas Dei" belongs in the context of this tradition. Thus, among Christian presuppositions, "prudentia," too, and not just knowing effective means in the political arena, is one of the great "virtues"; nor does church doctrine deny its relation to the holiness of mankind. Not until the beginning of modernity did this background disappear, and then "prudentia" came to be understood in a technical way, as mere knowledge of the right means. In this way, however, it ultimately became indistinguishable from what, according to Aristotle, is no ἀρετή, but rather a dubious facility (δεινότης) (*Nicomachean Ethics* Z 13, 1144a23 ff.).

Corresponding to this is Kant's distinction between the technical imperative of cleverness and the commands of morality. Behind it lies the distinction between the sense of causality and its categorical ontological value, the "causality of freedom." As is well known, for Kant freedom is no mere fact—that is, not a fact of scientific experience—but rather a fact of reason. The new opposition between is and ought that governs post-Kantian theory of science goes back to this distinction in Kant's moral philosophy. If something is a pure fact and of itself contains no relation whatever to the good, only then is it at the arbitrary disposal of reason. The realm of ought, within which the relation to the good is circumscribed, has to do not with facts but with "values."[1]

Thus, the realm of Ought and values was excluded from the knowable by Kant's followers in modern science. This finally led to the strict legalistic differentiation between so-called judgments of fact and "judgments of value," though it broke down entirely in the process of semantic evolution.

In the meantime, the earlier philosophy of "politics" was displaced by what went under the new designation of "political

science" or "politology." This change expresses the radical sci-
entization which led to the breakup of the Aristotelian metaphysical tradition in the age of modern science. A new concept of knowledge—"science"—took over. For this reason, in
the final chapter of his *Inductive Logic*, John Stuart Mill treats
traditional practical philosophy under the rubric of "the moral
sciences"—a kind of experimental science, though of a very
inexact sort. The German translation of this title—"Geisteswissenschaften"—drove its roots deep in Germany. In it one
can hear a different note than that of methodical science: it
is the heritage laid up in Hegel's concept of objective *Geist*.
Through it the modern concept of science was truly modi-
fied and enriched—dogmatists would say "watered down." The
Geisteswissenschaften are in truth not merely one department
of the sciences. Despite all "inexactness," they are the proper
bearers of the great burden of tradition, and they have found
their language in Hegel's concept of Geist and its avatars. In
other languages they live on as "humanities" or "letters."

Seen from this point of view, the imperative seems too narrow a starting point. The question arises as to whether duties
ought to play such a definitive role in ethics, and whether the
imperative can really be the whole of ethics. It is, of course,
actually only a part of the Stoic heritage that lives on from
classical antiquity. The Stoa taught people to withdraw from
everything that does not lie within our power. For otherwise
we are helplessly subject to the mutability of fortune and mis-
fortune. The Stoic ideal of equanimity thus ultimately implies,
too, withdrawal from all public things, as actually had to be the
case for the Greeks in the Hellenistic period and the age of the
Roman Caesars. What is more, that same withdrawal was considered appropriate to the modern scientific frame of mind, the
consequences of which led inevitably to the impasses of modern subjectivism.

The opposition of Is and Ought has certainly always been an aspect of morality. But only in modernity has it found its formulation. For only now is it the case that "is" (or today "the facts") lacks all relation to the good. In view of the narrowness of all imperative ethics, our gaze always needs to consider the whole of the moral-political world and therefore return to Aristotle, the founder of practical philosophy who also created a "teleological" physics that, for a millennium and a half, constituted physics as such. In Aristotle is to be found neither the concept of duty nor even a reasonable verbal equivalent for it, still less the concept of Should. He uses, it is true, a somewhat surprising Greek expression, which people are tempted to use for "should": ὡς δεῖ, "as is necessary." We find the word δέον in association with ἀγαθόν, the good, in the phrase ἀγαθὸν καὶ δέον ("good and binding"). δέον means the binding, the obligatory. It refers less to a demand that is made binding on single individuals than to a common basis of obligation on which are grounded all customs and forms of social life.

The later Stoic concept of καθῆκον—that which is due and suitable to someone—again sounds less like "should" than like "have." The change from καθῆκον and καλόν to Latin "officium," it seems to me, mirrors the decline of the free polis and the transition to increasing dependency and officialdom. This transition marked a new integration of Stoic thought into the life-world of the Roman republic, sacred and political, and it accorded the concept of duty its central role in ethics. It is only with Cicero that the word "officium" or "duty" comes into general usage. The German word "Pflicht" (duty) is a Germanization that originates in the eighteenth century, and Garvey's translation of Cicero's "officium" contributed to the formation of the concept of duty in which are still to be heard its Latin origins, the "official" and the presence of the political. Then, when Kant accepted and analyzed it, the concept of the imperative first took the further step of moving from grammar into ethics.

Here we are a long way from the sovereign realm of theoretical knowledge proper, as paradigmatically represented by the mathematical ideal of proof constructed by the Greeks. Even the so-called deontic logic, of which there is so much talk these days, does not in truth suffice to describe the logical structure valid for all *technical* thought. It remains decisively indebted to *practical* knowledge. So, too, the use to which Aristotle puts the so-called practical syllogism and the theory of logical conclusions in his *Ethics* shows that it is in fact always a technical syllogism. Of course, it is connected to the significant new beginning represented by modern mathematics itself. Since mathematics made possible the rise of modern natural science, altering modern experience of the world, syllogistic logic itself has entirely lost its scientific significance (one thinks of Liebig's critique of Bacon). The concept of science that begins with mathematics and governs Greek thought developed the logic of proof conceived as derivation from a first, the principle. Under the dominion of the universal, the individual became a case and, in modern natural science, a case of some natural law. Thereby it becomes impossible to do justice to the logic of research in the natural sciences and, in the realm of culture, to sufficiently legitimate practical philosophy as science, when necessary, in the cognitive and research domain of the so-called human sciences.

For this reason, the return to Aristotle acquires a new meaning. Aristotle became the founder of practical philosophy when —alongside the ideal of science, the "mathemata," and the "physics" that he had comprehensively elaborated—he erected practical philosophy entirely on its own footing, rather than treating it as a special form of theoretical philosophy. Aristotle is inquiring about the humanly good, which he expressly opposes to questions about the universal idea of the good that Plato's dialogues frequently put in the mouth of Socrates. When Plato unites the good of the soul, the good of the polis, and the good of the universe all together, this sublime Pythagorean world vision is erected upon the theoretical basis of numbers. This can afford no genuine satisfaction to human life, grappling with its tasks, striving for its goals, and searching for happiness—as confirmed by the famous anecdote about Plato's lecture "on the Good" and its reception by the Attic public. In his polemical counterposition, Aristotle erects practical philosophy not on the universal idea of the good; his starting point (principle, ἀρχή, the first) is rather the "that" (Daß, τὸ ὅτι).

This is not to be understood as some fact that could be determined, a "factum brutum." What the moral disposition, and especially the disposition of philosophy, is grounded on, when it is concerned to open up the moral dimension, is much more the understanding among people that they always already possess by reason of their life and their life together. In Greek society was realized a whole series of life projects that Aristotle enters into (Nicomachean Ethics A 3).[3] There is hedonism, projecting gay merriment as the end of life. There is the project of pragmatic success as the goal of political life, fulfilled in the honors heaped on one. Finally, there is a projective orientation that completely transcends everything purposeful. This is projection toward the καλόν, the beautiful, which is free of all calculation and therefore good "in itself." Thus the "arete" is good in itself—whether someone envisions his highest goal as action or observation. This is what is meant by taking the "that" as one's starting point. It is based on the self-projection of human Dasein. It has nothing in common with the ideal of demonstrable knowledge or deriving the special from the general. The desire for grounding and the ideal of certainty view themselves as situated within a completely different forum. Yet the pressure of the demonstrative proof that runs up against its limit in arete still shows up everywhere in the philosophy of our time. It shows up in the expression "ultimate foundation," which Husserl himself took up in order to bend the knee and affiliate his conception of phenomenological research with German Idealism's concept of system and its neo-Kantian successors. But can ethics or practical philosophy receive such scientific grounding or justification at all? Given the demands of the situation they involve, would not the mere application of the universal to the individual case put a false burden on them, instead of encouraging people to make responsible decisions? As if this realm had to do with following rules!

Must we not, however, pose the question in a more general manner? What task can philosophy perform at all in the realm of moral and political praxis? This is the real question that life asks of practical philosophy. Philosophical reflection is a theoretical movement of thought. The kind of reflection that practical philosophy involves must nonetheless raise a claim with inner necessity, not only to know what the good is but contribute to it. In any case, a person wants to know what is best for the purpose of making a decision—whether commission or omission. It is from this point of view that one must understand the fundamental question of practical philosophy that arises in the age of universal science, as Aristotle's interpretation of the world tries to be, and even in the age of modern science. Our task is therefore doubled—not just to make ourselves aware of the world orientation that Aristotle projects and thus necessarily bring our own concepts into play. It is equally necessary to take up Kant's moral philosophy once again and see what is right about it. For in the era of modern science, brilliantly illuminated by the ideals of the modern Enlightenment, Kant once again discovered the fundamental question of practical philosophy.

Kant himself said that Rousseau put him right. His grounding of the "categorical imperative" did not serve the purpose of opening up a new realm of sovereign self-governance for the autonomous subject. Quite the opposite, contrary to the presumption of a universal, scientifically grounded pragmatism in life, its purpose was to ground moral obligation on moral freedom. To be sure, what is here called grounding and founding cannot mean the same thing as do grounds and foundations in theoretical explanations. As Kant has shown, freedom is not a fact of theoretical reason that can be proved. It is a fact of reason one must assume if one is to consider oneself a human being. To attempt a proof of freedom is just as mistaken in Kant's eyes as in Aristotle's eyes it is mistaken to derive ethics from the highest principle of the good. Kant's *Foundation of the Metaphysics of Morals,* his most profound work of moral philosophy, expressly raises the question of what philosophical reflection can do at all in a domain where the human heart and the subtlety of the human conscience require an exactitude of self-examination and consideration that is nowhere exceeded. Thus in Kant, as in Aristotle, it is not a matter of grounding moral obligation conceptually through theoretical reflection. Morality and ethics do not require exceptional intellectual talents or a capacity for highly educated thinking. What, then, can possibly legitimate philosophical reflection's claim to be of practical advantage to human moral existence, as philosophy still plainly maintains? The answer lies in the fact that people always already subordinate their concrete decisions to general goals—though usually rather unclearly—and thus they are engaging in practical philosophy. This explains what right thinking should be. Kant's *Foundation of the Metaphysics of Morals,* we see, offers an answer to this question.

Aristotle was well aware of the fact that practical philosophy can do nothing but pursue the drive toward knowledge and self-understanding that is always manifesting itself in human actions and decisions; it can do nothing but raise vague intuitions to greater clarity—as aiming toward a particular point helps the archer hit the target (*Nicomachean Ethics A* 1, 1093a23 f.) or through more exact analysis of a goal already known to one (*Eudemian Ethics A* 2, 1214b11).

The situation of Germany at the end of the First World War was specially suited to raising these questions. Under the leadership of Husserl, and thanks to his patience and mastery of description, the phenomenological school had reacquired the horizon of the life-world and shown that we needed to get behind and beyond the horizon of science and the epistemological glare that flooded it and the entire nineteenth century. Knowledge of the life-world is always a furthering and development of a mode of deliberation that is rooted in life itself and unfolds in life practice. Thus, it can only be practical knowledge that is in question here, whether this "virtue" of knowing is called deliberation, circumspection, discretion, or "prudentia." The critique that Kierkegaard had earlier directed at Hegel's totalizing dialectical synthesis now began to influence phenomenology's disposition toward illuminating the life-world in itself. It can be shown that, whatever the differences, it was just this motif to which Aristotle and Kant had attempted to give conceptual expression.

The critique of the liberal period's faith in science availed itself of Kierkegaard's concept of "existence" as it had been deployed in opposition to Hegel's all-mediating synthesis. Now, in our century, the point is not, of course, to produce another critique of Hegel's speculative idealism. Rather, the issue now is the epistemological methodologism of the reigning neo-Kantianism. In that connection, people began to ask what rationality really is, as it operates in the clarity of the practical life of humanity and distinguishes itself, apparently fundamentally, from the theoretical rationality of science. In answering this question, Aristotle can be helpful—perhaps even more than Kierkegaard. Indeed, the whole of Aristotle's ethics is governed by the question about the ἄλλο εἶδος γνώσεως, the "other kind of knowledge" that life itself is concerned with.[2]

At this point a hermeneutic consideration must be introduced. We would be falling into a naive dogmatism if we compelled all the texts that have been preserved for us by the accidents of ancient tradition to assume the reflective level of modern scientific literature. Neither Plato's dialogues nor Aristotle's textbooks belong to this category. The dialogues of Plato accord us broad knowledge of Plato's thought, even though Aristotle and other later sources offer us critical assessments of Plato's thought and doctrine. This is not at all altered by the fact that the dialogues are conducted in imitation of the style of Socrates and afford only limited opportunity for the language of concepts. By contrast, Aristotle is concerned with constructing concepts. Even so, Aristotelian ethics takes on the task of reformulating the usages of living language in the language of concepts. Thus Aristotle sets out—especially in his theory of intellectual virtues, the "dianoetic virtues"—by examining five expressions that in Plato are all synonymous; that is, they are used entirely without differentiation. These are techne, *episteme*, phronesis, nous, and *sophia*. Aristotle characterizes these five concepts as ἕξεις τοῦ ἀληθεύειν, modes of being of knowing-being (*Seinsweisen des Wissendseins*) or securing the true (*Verwahren des Wahren*). All forms of knowing that are mere acceptance or viewpoint or opinion cannot really be called knowing, because they admit error. The five modes of knowledge are five forms of reliability, as opposed to all mistake and concealment. It can be shown that of these five, only "sophia" (wisdom) and "phronesis" (practical reason) are for Aristotle truly "best," true virtues.

For insight into the central significance[3] of this analysis of the dianoetic virtues, I am indebted to Heidegger's Freiburg seminar of the summer semester of 1923. Clearly the searching analysis of the concepts thus expressed ultimately serves the purpose of distinguishing phronesis, the special kind of practical knowledge, from other forms of being known that find their realization in fulfilling theoretical and technical ends.

Let us begin with the Greek expression λόγον ἔχειν. This is an expression commonly used in a theoretical as well as a practical sense. Λόγον ἔχειν can mean "to have proof." This is best illustrated by the mathematical ideal of science. For the Greeks, in fact, mathematics became the very first science, because of its ideal of proof and logic of proof, and precisely because of its logic of proof the Greeks made the mathematical knowledge of the Egyptians and Babylonians into science. This is confirmed in the third part of the sixth book of the *Nicomachean Ethics,* which describes the concept of "episteme" in terms of mathematics, especially those of later Euclidian geometry. Episteme is a mode of being known that depends on having proofs.

Now, there is also a different meaning of λόγον ἔχειν, a moral meaning to which Aristotle consciously alludes, both in the thirteenth part of the first book and in the first and second sections of book VI of the *Nicomachean Ethics.* Λόγον ἔχειν means "to be answerable," and is also used to describe the way one listens to one's father—that is, with respect. Respect is not being blindly subject to the will of another. It is rather participation in the superiority of a knowledge that is recognized to be authoritative. To give respect does not mean acceding to another against one's own convictions, but rather allowing one's own convictions to be codetermined by another. In Aristotle this becomes clear precisely in the detailed analysis he dedicates to the formation of right convictions and thus making right decisions, which he terms "prohairesis." Precisely this defines the free behavior of the practical-moral person who is a citizen of a city. (Slaves have no prohairesis.)

We need to protect ourselves from the dogmatism of doxographic school examinations. Hermeneutics teaches us to pay attention to the difference between a philosophical textbook and, on the other hand, a literary work of art, such as the Socratic dialogues of Plato. This becomes apparent in the treatment given to the parts of the soul in the two forms of verbal tradition, in Aristotle and in Plato. In Plato's *Republic* the doctrine of the parts of the soul is extensively developed. There it ultimately serves the purpose of demonstrating the unity of the soul in the plurality of its members and likewise the unity of the polis, where well-being of the soul as well as that of the city depends on the harmony of voices. Nothing is so terrible as a civil war or a person who is terribly rent apart. In Plato's mythical analogues, we often read how the soul is inwardly threatened with becoming split, and how everything depends on the unity of mutual accord. From time immemorial, the Greeks considered the labyrinth of the human heart to be like the horrors of civil war. When in the *Nicomachean Ethics* Aristotle avails himself of the concept of the λόγον ἔχειν, the ἄλογον, and so on, and downplays the difference between them, it is in no sense a criticism. There he employs the elegant image of the difference between convex and concave, which illustrates that one and the same thing can be described in various ways, and the whole difference consists in the manner of description. The soul is as much one and the same as a curve, though it is viewed from one side as caved out and from the other as bowed out. Thus in *De anima* (*B* 4) Aristotle explicitly insists on the fact that parts of the soul do not exist in the same sense as parts of the body, its members and organs. Instead, the soul exists as one and presents itself as the one which it is in terms of its various possibilities.

This is something we ought to take to heart, according to Aristotle. The distinction between ethical virtues and dianoetic virtues that we meet with there has a methodological meaning. Aristotle wants to show unequivocally that there is no phronesis without ethos and no ethos without phronesis. The two of them are both aspects of the same basic constitution of humanity. We have prohairesis, we must choose. We have free choice, but we are not free not to choose. Thus Aristotle can say of prohairesis that it is an impulse that involves thought or, alternatively, that it is a thought that involves impulse (ὄρεξις διανοητική or διάνοια ὀρεκτική: *Nicomachean Ethics Z* 2, 1139b5). It is completely mistaken to divorce this kind of thought (and thus knowledge) from ethos. The whole subject of phronesis is discussed in answer to the question what it really means to describe ethos as something that contains logos.

What is logos? Aristotle takes up the question in full cognizance of the Socratic heritage. He emphasizes that virtue is behaving *with* logos and that this means not only that our behavior corresponds to a logos, a law (κατὰ τὸν λόγον). Rather, it means that this behavior is μετὰ τοῦ λόγου—that is, it does not just correspond to thought but has thought in the very midst of it.

Aristotle then sets himself to the immense task of differentiating this thought, this form of knowing, this knowledge involved in the phronesis that guides practice, from the other forms of knowing where, for instance, theoretical knowledge or cognitively dominated production and manual skill are involved. In such conceptual formulations, Aristotle tries to follow the hints offered by linguistic usage. Thus the noun φρόνησις, like the adjective φρόνιμος, is to be met with primarily in pragmatic contexts, where it means reasonableness and good sense. "Phronesis" thus is distinct from "sophia" (or σοφός) and especially from "episteme," which I called knowing-being (*Wissendsein*).

Such conceptual formulations are not, of course, rules binding linguistic usage. In the life-world where language is used, these expressions often overlap each other, as they even do in Plato as well. For just this reason, Aristotle undertook this conceptual analysis, and it is quite clear that he sought to pick up from language things for which he still lacked proper conceptual means.

The concept of "synesis" (semantically close to phronesis) illustrates this very nicely. In German we might call it "Verständnis" (being understanding). We, too, can discern a virtue in someone's being understanding. When we say this in German—probably other languages have equivalent expressions—we do not really mean that someone understands or comprehends another person well, but rather that he is trying to understand the other—and that means really understand "him." But in Greek usage, the word σύνεσις is used primarily for the ability to learn—that is, the mere capacity to comprehend in the theoretical realm. In the *Nicomachean Ethics*, by contrast, Aristotle is looking for another kind of knowing, one that determines the practical behavior and being of humanity. Thus he situates *synesis* in the context of a series, climaxing in phronesis, designating the kinds of political and human concern for the good and for "arete." Into this same series go things like γνώμη (insight) and συγγνώμη (forbearance). Thus Aristotle unmistakably defines the whole series of φρόνησις, σύνεσις, γνώμη, συγγνώμη by reference to ἄλλο εἶδος γνώσεως, that other kind of knowing that is obviously not merely a kind of knowing, but rather a knowing that arises from the being of humankind, its human nature, its character, the way one's whole human demeanor is formed. This is the knowing that Aristotle is looking for and that is determinative for human life, its well-being and good fortune. With this, imperatives in the proper sense of the word have nothing whatever to do.

Now we need to determine what Kant's contribution is and

relate it to our question. There can be no doubt that Kant was not the inventor of the theory of duties. On the contrary. He worked within an already fully developed tradition of duties that must ultimately be considered a Stoic, not a Mosaic, tradition. The concept of duty basically describes the simple obviousness which those of solidly founded character ascribe to the maxims of behavior they solidly maintain. It therefore plays no founding role, as the first section of Kant's *Foundation* shows. Kant's concern was to define the essence of moral reason on which all obligation is founded. We have already seen that he did not undertake to found the whole of moral self-determination upon the omnipotence and authority of subjectivity—as preeminently Fichte understood him to do, as well as Schiller, probably even Reinhold, and at any rate the whole post-Kantian tradition.

Kant, we recall, uses the expression "autonomy." Gerhard Krüger has shown,[4] in a book that has been insufficiently read and pondered, that "autonomy" is not meant to ground the origin and validity of a moral law, for example. It is what should guide in judging what is the case for me. It belongs to the typic of "judgment" that Kant himself discusses in this context in the *Critique of Practical Reason*. It merely refers to a kind of clarification that serves our judgment when we want to determine what the moral law demands in this case. "Autonomy" explains the capacity for generalizing in our maxims and the absence of exceptions implied in the concept of the law. This is clarified by comparison with the law of nature, with social codifications, and with the metaphysical realm of ends. Thus the "typus" of autonomy needs to be understood as being directed against the tendency of human nature which Kant describes at the end of the first section of the *Foundation* as the sophistry of passion and the inclination to rationalize. Here Kant begins from the position that, in themselves, virtue and righteousness could not be something attainable by a heightened capacity for understanding or even conceptual clarity and precision. The Enlightenment's hubristic presumption is to believe that humanity can be perfected by means of its understanding and science. The moral progress of humankind, insofar as it is possible to speak of such a thing at all, must be viewed as something other than the rise of human knowledge and ability. Now it is the case that reason is so much at work in each human being, even in his moral deliberations, that he is always tempted to use this very reason to resist the obligation of what is known to be right in a given field. This is what Kant means by "rationalizing." One probably recognizes that the moral law is obligatory, but in special cases one tries to find reasons for making an exception. The point, then, is to prevent the "dialectic of the exception" that at once considers something valid and yet excepts itself from it. This is exactly the same thing as is manifest in the other models that Kant's formulations of the categorical imperative employ—natural law and juridical law—and it should be compellingly manifest in what is perhaps the most enduring definition of morality that Kant found: namely, that one ought never to use another person as a means, but always acknowledge as well that he is an end in himself. This fundamental law of humanity, probably Christian culture's finest bequest to humankind, is today just as clearly evident as are natural and juridical law by reason of their own definitions.

It is therefore quite mistaken to relate Kant's famous critique of eudaimonism to the great tradition of practical philosophy that begins with Aristotle's founding of this discipline. Kant too considers it natural for human beings to concern themselves with their well-being and good fortune. Now, for Aristotle there is no question but that virtue would obey the demands of the moral as a means to the end of such well-being. It is not superior worldly wisdom that Aristotle is recommending when he defines virtue as the middle path between evils. To be sure, it belongs to the nature of human beings to strive for their own well-being, insofar as they are not required by a higher duty to check their own inclinations, specifically out of concern for the other and observance of the "moral law." The eudaimonism that Kant criticizes, on the other hand, suggests that by worldly wisdom one should so arrange things that one's highest well-being is achieved, and so-called good fortune thereby acquired. Against this assertion, and considering the obvious multiplicity of human visions of happiness, Kant summoned up the critical idea of the universal *categorical* imperative. His position can be rightly understood only if it is seen in polemical opposition to the Enlightenment thinking of the time. He is not offering to ground morality, but to defend it against the doubts originating from the Enlightenment's cognitive pride, as criticized by Rousseau. In this respect Kant stands behind the ambition and brilliance of his followers. They extended the primacy of practical reason to the realm of theoretical knowledge, and thereby to the whole modern culture of science, beginning with Galileo and his followers, and subordinated it yet again to the primacy of the concept of purpose, thus giving primacy to practical reason even in the theoretical use of reason. We are indebted to them for an immense number of anthropological and moral insights. Yet we cannot overlook the fact that the genuine task of reason, among its highly various cognitive tasks, is not fulfilled by making action consistent with scientific knowledge. When we try to derive and confirm the results of research in the natural sciences a priori from a teleological viewpoint, we conceal the researcher's tasks, tasks that require humane knowledge and humane ability, and that are required of us all in the interest of the good and thus too of human life together on this earth. Despite all criticism of the narrowness of Kant's distinctions, he is right about the main thing: validating the moral task in

the face of the ever growing expansion of scientific and technological power. Therein Kant seems to me to have best preserved
our own heritage with respect to German Idealism in all its
wealth. In carrying out the research that is its charge, the world
of science cannot consider itself as attempting to satisfy human
purposes. (Nor can science as such succeed in doing so without thereby betraying itself and handing itself over to political
dependency.) That is the task, rather, of all people and their
practical reason. Humanity will survive if it succeeds in bringing the vast destructive potential that science has placed in our
hands under control by means of a superior reasonableness, a
"phronesis" in the Aristotelian sense. Political pressure cannot
do so, because it is always tempted toward the misuse of power.

Lately people have sometimes spoken of the two worlds in
which we find ourselves: the world of natural science and the
other world represented by human culture in all its riches; and
the British writer C. P. Snow, who first coined this critical
notion, still seriously believed that he needed to decry the deficiency of scientific knowledge in the cultural life of humanity.
He was deeply mistaken if he thought he recognized, as well,
a weakness in the education offered by the elite British uni-
versities of the time. The question is not whether human
facilities, and thus the achievements of science in making our
world known, also find sufficient reception in the minds of
humanity. The opposite is the real-life question for human
beings: whether we will succeed in tying the immense increase
in human power to reasonable ends and integrating it into a
reasonable system of life. This will never occur merely by increasing human power, but only through insight and the increasing solidarity between people as it has been conceptualized
via the heritage of Aristotle's practical philosophy and paral-
leled in the great religions, as well as in other cultural circles.

Kant's special accomplishment was in part to have understood how to conceive of religion "within the limits of reason alone," and thereby to have pointed out the paths in a pluralistically fragmented world whereby we can take a step further toward the dream of eternal peace.

Notes

CHAPTER 2
On the Possibility of a Philosophical Ethics

1. Kant, *Grundlegung zur Metaphysik der Siften* (Berlin, 1902), 4:404 ff.
2. Hegel, *Phenomenologie der Geist,* ed. J. Hoffmeister (Leipzig and Hamburg, 1905), pp. 301 ff.
3. G. Krüger, *Philosophie und Moral in der Kantischen Kritik* (Tübingen, 1931; 2d ed., 1967).
4. As the editor of the *Walberger Studien* remarks, Thomas Aquinas emphasizes that "conscience" refers to an act, and only in an extended sense to a habitus underlying it (*Summa theologica* 1:79, 13; vol. 6).
5. Underlying my discussion here is my essay "Praktisches Wissen" of 1930, which has been published for the first time in my *Gesammelte Werke* (Tübingen, 1985-95), 5:230 ff.
6. *Nicomachean Ethics Z* 5, 1140b17: εὐθὺς οὐ φαίνεται ἡ ἀρχή.
7. Ibid., *B* 3, 1105b12 ff.: ἐπὶ τὸν λόγον καταφεύγοντες.
8. See my essay "Freundschaft und Selbsterkenntnis," in the *Festschrift* for U. Höllscher: *Würzburger Abhandlungen zur Altertumswissenschaft* NF 1 (1985): 25-33 (*Gesammelte Werke,* 7:396-406).
9. See my review of Gauthier-Jolif's commentary on the *Nicomachean Ethics,* in *Philosophische Rundschau* 10 (1962): 293 ff. (*Gesammelte Werke,* 6:302-6).
10. More on this in *Truth and Method,* rev. ed., trans. Joel Weinsheimer and Donald G. Marshall (New York, 1992), pp. 318 ff. (*Gesammelte Werke,* 1:324 ff., 2:401 ff.).
11. Plato, *Republic* 302a.

CHAPTER 3
On the Divine in Early Greek Thought

1. W. Jaeger, *Die Theologie der früheren griechischen Denker* (Stuttgart, 1953), p. 43.
2. Karl Reinhardt, *Parmenides* (Bonn, 1916), pp. 251 f.
3. Bruno Snell, *Die Entdeckung des Geistes* (Hamburg, 1946), pp. 205 f.

4. H. Boeder has elaborated on this in *Grund und Gegenwart als Frageziel der frühgriechischen Philosophie* (The Hague, 1962).

5. *Metaphysics* Λ 8, 1074b1 ff.

6. Ibid., *B* 4, 1000a9 ff.

7. The cardinal mistake in Werner Jaeger's brilliant analysis of the "Theologie der frühen Griechen," I think, is that he reverses this relationship. The same is the case for O. Gigon's careful and prudent lecture to be seen in the Fondation Hardt; the appendix especially, in my opinion, addresses a question to the tradition that is inappropriate to it. Does this "theology" of the Ionians and Eleatics have anything at all to do with the factical religion of the time?

8. Karl Joël, *Der Ursprung der Naturphilosophie aus dem Geiste der Mystik* (Jena, 1906).

9. F. M. Cornford, *Principium Sapientiae: The Origins of Greek Philosophical Thought* (Cambridge, 1952).

10. Plato, *Sophist* 248e8.

11. Gadamer, "Vorgestalten der Reflexion," in *Subjectivität und Metaphysik, Festschrift* for W. Cramer (Frankfurt am Main, 1966), pp. 128–43 (*Gesammelte Werke* 6:116–28).

12. See H. J. Krämer, *Der Ursprung der Geistmetaphysik* (Amsterdam, 1964), pp. 193 ff. There Krämer admittedly completely exceeds the immanent interpretation of the conversation and tries to answer on new ground a question that is completely unanswerable from it—namely, whether the transcendent world of Ideas or the "totality" is meant by παντελῶς ὄν. This question is irrelevant to the dialogic theme of the Sophist. No more can the philosopher follow the Heracliteans than those who accept the one *or* the many Ideas. Parmenides and a dogmatic Platonism are equally valid! Thus the "dynamic character of Plato's cosmos of ideas" merely interpolates a new dogmatism into a conversation that was trying to answer for the first time the question about what it is that is here called "dynamic"—to become at one with ὄν and μὴ ὄν through knowledge of the structure of the λόγος.

13. *Laws* X, 898d ff. is a certain proof of this, as Jaeger has already seen.

14. *De caelo* B13, 294a30 f.

15. *Fragmente der Vorsokratiker* (hereafter *VS*), (Berlin, 1906) 2, A 2.

16. See Boeder, *Grund und Gegenwart*.

17. *VS* 18 B 8, 4 and 8, 42–9 with *VS* 20 B 2 and b 4.

18. Instead, it follows from the demiurge's intention that he leave nothing out of the four elements that he brings together (*Timaeus* 32c, 33a)—and even that is still criticized as a representation that is much too extrinsic,

because with respect to the σῶμα, the soul is first. It is only with Aristotle, who dissolves the myth of the demiurge and recognizes only the (σύνολον), that the argument from the ὕλη receives full weight.

19. The dominant role that this aspect of the *Timaeus* has played from Xenocrates on, that finally led to shifting the ideas into the divine spirit, we can now see thanks to the investigations of P. Merlan, *From Platonism to Neoplatonism* (The Hague, 1953) and more clearly of H. J. Krämer (*Der Ursprung*). Of course, with the exception of Aristotle, the Academy translated the Timaeus myth into serious doctrine in the style of a compact theology. What this means is a problem of a general kind that I have examined in another context. (See "Begriffsgeschichte als Philosophie," *Archiv für Begriffsgeschichte* 14 [1970]; *Gesammelte Schriften*, 2:77-91.)

20. Even Proclos recognizes the logical function of the "divine art," though on the basis of an artificial interpretation of 31a (κατὰ τὸ παράδειγμα δεδημιουργημένος). See E. Diehl, ed., *Procli Diadochi in Platonis Timaeum Commentaria* (Lipsiae, 1903), 133d.

21. Not only Krämer (see n. 19 above) but many others argue thus.

22. The extent to which the concept of life colors the concept of the whole can be seen further from Aristotle's summary passage in *Metaphysics* Δ 27, 1024a11 f., where the ὅλον, the maimed, succeeds the κολοβόν, the whole.

23. Theophrastus, *Metaphysics* 5b.

CHAPTER 4
The Ontological Problem of Value

1. Hegel, *Phenomenologie der Geist*, ed. Hoffmeister (Leipzig and Hamburg, 1905), pp. 423 ff.: "Der seiner selbst gewisse Geist."

2. H. Lotze, *Kleine Schriften* (Leipzig, 1885-91), 3:305.

3. H. Lotze, *Mikrokosmos* (Leipzig, 1856-64), 2:416.

4. Ibid., p. 276.

5. Friedrich Nietzsche, *Gesammelte Werke* (Munich, 1920-29), 8:338.

6. Alois Roth, *Edmund Husserls ethische Untersuchungen: Dargestellt anhand seiner Vorlesungsmanuskripte* (The Hague, 1960).

7. Ibid., p. 105.

8. N. Hartman, *Ethik* (Berlin, 1916), pp. 227 ff.

9. M. Scheler, foreword to 3d ed. of *Materiale Wertethik*; now in Scheler's *Gesammelten Werken* (Munich, 1966), 2:21.

CHAPTER 5

Thinking as Redemption: Plotinus between Plato and Augustine

1. Ferdinand Christian Bauer, *Die christliche Gnosis* (Tübingen, 1835). And later, Hans Jonas, *Gnosis und spätantiker Geist* (Göttingen, 1934).

2. In this context it is significant that Proclus's commentary on Plato's *Parmenides* considers only the dialogue's first hypothesis, which was accessible for such interpretation. On this see my "Der platonische *Parmenides* und seine Nachwirkung," in *Gesammelte Werke* (Tübingen, 1991), 7:313-27.

3. Compare my remarks on the concept of the spring in Appendix 5 of *Truth and Method*, trans. Joel Weinsheimer and Donald Marshall (New York, 1989), pp. 501-2.

4. Fortunate first made, Creation's spoiled darlings,
   mountain ranges, peaks reddened by the first of all suns, — pollen
   of a blossoming God,
   pivots of light, corridors, stairways, thrones, spaces formed of sheer
   Being, shields of ecstasy, resounding
   tempests of rapture, and suddenly, every one, *mirrors:* drawing back
   into your own faces
   the same beauty you brilliantly beamed out.
   The Duino Elegies, trans. Leslie Norris and Alan Keele
   (Columbia, SC, 1993), "Second Elegy," p. 9.

CHAPTER 6

Myth in the Age of Science

1. On this topic see the first two of my Hölderlin studies in *Gesammelte Werke,* vol. 9: "Hölderlin und die Antike" and "Hölderlin und das Zukünftige."

2. Christian Hartlich and Walter Sachs, *Der Ursprung des Mythosbegriffes in der modernen Bibelwissenschaft* (Tübingen, 1952).

3. Introduction to *Philosophie der Mythology,* in *Sämtliche Werke,* ed. K. F. A. Schelling (Stuttgart and Augsburg, 1856), 11:193.

4. Ibid., p. 198.

5. On the problem of applying this concept to Greek religion, see my essay "Sokrates' Frömmigkeit des Nichtwissens," in my *Gesammelte Werke,* 7:83-117.

6. Walter F. Otto, *Die Götter Griechenlands* (Bonn, 1929); *Dionysos: Mythos und Kultus* (Frankfurt, 1933).